The
White House
Boys

The
White House
Boys

An American Tragedy

Roger Dean Kiser

Health Communications, Inc.
Deerfield Beach, Florida

www.hcibooks.com

Permissions

Carol Marbin Miller, "Reform school alumni recount beatings, rapes" from
The Miami Herald (October 19, 2008). Copyright © 2008 by McClatchy
Company. Reproduced with permission of McClatchy Company via Copy-
right Clearance Center.

Brendan Farrington, "Unknown graves at Fla. reform school investigated."
Copyright © 2008 by Associated Press. All rights reserved. Reprinted with
permission.

Tallahassee Democrat, editorial, "Our Opinion: Memories of state abuse can't
be erased" (October 23, 2008). Reprinted by permission of the Tallahassee
Democrat. All rights reserved.

Library of Congress Cataloging-in-Publication Data
is available through the Library of Congress.

Publisher: Health Communications, Inc.
           3201 S.W. 15th Street
           Deerfield Beach, FL 33442-8190

R-02-09

Cover images from the Florida Archives
Cover design by Larissa Hise Henoch
Interior design by Lawna Patterson Oldfield
Interior formatting by Andrea Perrine Brower

*To all those who had very little to share
but shared what little they had with me anyway.
In doing so, they taught me the meaning of
goodness, kindness, and generosity, providing me
with the foundation for a meaningful life.*

"If nature intended for me to be who I am,
then why did the system try to beat me
into something I am not?"

—*Roger Dean Kiser*

Contents

PART TWO: THE CHILD NOW SPEAKS AS A MAN

APPENDICES

Prologue

I f you were to drive down a long, narrow, winding grassy road, hidden far from sight, deep in the beautiful, thick underbrush of the north Florida woods, you will find unmarked graves containing the remains of thirty-two bodies, most likely all boys, some possibly as young as nine. As of now, who they are and how they got there is a mystery.

It is believed that some of those boys were beaten to death in the name of discipline. Some suspect that many more bodies might be scattered about somewhere in the murky, shallow swamplands and fields of the lush state of Florida.

The United States Department of Justice, along with the Federal Bureau of Investigation, is investigating the allegations to determine the truth about a deep, dark secret that has been hidden for almost fifty years.

A Florida State juvenile facility set up for the safety and rehabilitation of children went totally awry, virtually from the time the doors opened in January 1900, basically becoming a concentration camp for wayward boys. It is only recently that the abuse—physical, mental, and sexual—suffered by the children at the Florida Industrial School for Boys is being taken seriously, now that so many of the survivors (many of them in their sixties) have stepped forward and banded together. The insane cruelty and alleged murders have been ignored or covered up by the authorities for more than fifty years . . . but no more.

One of the most horrendous places at the juvenile facility was a building known as the "White House"—which was later dubbed the "White House Torture Chamber." This building, which still stands today, is a small white concrete building where boys were whipped and beaten mercilessly for trying to run away or for breaking one of the many other rules, rules so strict that the boys were afraid, in some cases, to look at someone in charge "the wrong way." Without fences, gates, or perimeter guards, the fear of being sent to this torture chamber was the only means the state had to control the young "inmates."

The beatings many of the boys suffered were beyond brutal. Some were beaten so badly that when they returned from the White House, it was hard to tell who they were. Of course, treatment this brutal instilled fear into each and every boy incarcerated at the facility.

Mind you now, White House beatings weren't only for very serious offenses such as running away. Perhaps that was the original purpose. However, a time soon followed when beatings and whippings or threats of beatings and whippings were handed out for smoking, talking back, cursing, not making your bed correctly, not wearing a smile on your face, smiling too much, eating too slowly, not walking fast enough, stepping off the path, accidentally tripping in line, coughing, sharing food, dropping a pat of butter on the floor, or eating a blackberry off a bush while on a work detail. Sometimes, there was no reason. And sometimes . . . boys never made it out of the White House alive, or at least they were never seen or heard from again.

From the Florida Archives

The unmarked graves, date unknown.

Photo by R. Kiser

The unmarked graves, 2008.

Foreword

I've published a free e-mail newsletter called Heartwarmers.com for over ten years, sharing original short stories with people all over the world.

It's a little like prospecting for gold—I never know what is going to turn up in my e-mail inbox. While most submissions never get published, I read every one and love to discover new talent. I've taken pride in being able to help launch a few literary careers.

On June 21, 1999, I had the pleasure and privilege of introducing a new writer to our online community: Roger Kiser.

I have absolutely no idea how Roger stumbled upon Heartwarmers or what inspired him to send in a story. But as soon as I read it, I knew things would be different and lives would be touched— mine, our readers', and most of all, Roger's.

It didn't take long for Roger to find his voice and become one of our most beloved authors. Every time we published one of his stories, people from around the world would respond with appreciative e-mails. Now, no one would accuse Roger of being a sophisticated writer, or as Roger would say himself, "I don't write fancy-like." If anything, it's his writing simplicity that gives him a unique ability to take his readers with him—to another time and place—that instantly brands him as a special talent.

While Roger's writing style is one thing, the content of his stories puts him in an entirely different class. His memories of a gut-wrenching childhood, growing up in a cruel orphanage in northern Florida, was enough to cause his fellow orphans to journey down paths of self-destruction. And considering the tortures and atrocities that were thrust upon them, who could blame them?

But Roger emerged from the ashes in a different way. Yes, he had his share of run-ins with the law and a slew of failed relationships along the way. But despite the real-life experiences you will read in this shocking book—somehow, someway, there was a flame of justice and passion that was never extinguished from Roger's heart. That's what makes his life and writings so special.

You've heard of overcoming hardships and obstacles. You've heard of the strength of the human spirit over adversity. You've heard of people facing insurmountable odds and walking away victorious. However, nothing you have seen or heard will ever compare with what you are about to read. Hollywood couldn't make this up.

When you finish this book and your mind has had a chance to absorb the events that took place, you will ask yourself the same questions that thousand of my readers have continued to ask throughout the years: "How could Roger have survived? And what's inside him that allows him to still see the good in the world?"

You see, this book isn't about despair. It isn't about what evil people did to innocent children in what is considered a civilized country. It's not even about the White House, which has been closed forever and today stands silently as a tomb to the horrors committed within its walls.

This book is about hope.

In this day and age, when we are cynical and skeptical, eager to latch on to anything that can rescue us from depressing news, Roger's testimony provides all of us a lifeboat of strength and determination.

Roger reveals himself—scars and all—and in the process enables us to believe that it really is possible to see through the clouds, our everyday heartaches, and the dark forces that want to drag us down.

He isn't a reality TV show survivor. He's a real-life survivor! You will be astonished when you find out what Roger went through. And yet today, Roger is a living testament to the adage that good conquers evil.

He says, "From birth to age sixteen, I had been abandoned, sexually molested, beaten, cursed, and discarded as an unnecessary item. I had been taught and made to feel that I was nothing more than a worthless piece of shit. For the next fifty years, it was very difficult for me to find anything decent to think, or say, about humankind. . . . It was only through my grandchildren that I came to realize what the term 'love' meant and what a wonderful feeling it was to share such a marvelous thing with my fellowman. Even to this day, I am amazed that it took nothing more than several small, innocent children to save me."

While Roger's grandchildren may have saved

him, I say, "Roger, you have saved us!" And for that, thousands of people around the world will be forever grateful for his inspiration.

I am proud to call him my friend.

—*Lee Simonson*

Acknowledgments

I would like to begin by acknowledging the first two people in my life ever to show me any form of love: George Victor and Rozzie Eloise Usher. They took me into their home on numerous occasions. Without learning from their example, I would never have developed a sense of direction and would most likely be dead today or locked away somewhere in a deep, dark prison cell. Though their love was freely given, I did not appreciate or even realize the importance of what they had given me until I was almost forty years old. That is when I first began to realize that they had actually saved me. Let there be no doubt that the good qualities I possess as a person are the direct result of their love and kindness.

I also owe much to my wife, Judy. She herself was abused as a child and undertook a great responsibility when she took on a very dysfunctional Roger Dean Kiser fifteen years ago. We've grown together over the years and are on a journey toward healing.

From birth to age sixteen, I had been abandoned, sexually molested, beaten, cursed, and discarded. I had been taught that I was nothing more than a worthless piece of shit. For the next fifty years, I had difficulty finding anything positive about humankind as a whole. But as time went by, with Judy's help, I began to fit the pieces of the puzzle together, and she stood by me through thick and thin. I am certain that who I am now as a husband, father, and grandfather is the direct result of her strength, love, and devotion. I owe her more than I could ever repay.

I also have to give much credit to my children, Roger, James, Kevin, and Twila, for forgiving me for the many mistakes I made as a father. Though I never abused my children, I was not a loving man. I had yet to learn such feelings. I was kind and did the best I could with what little knowledge I had been given by my "caretakers."

It was only through my grandchildren—who I acknowledge now—Chelsey, Madison, Jane, Stephen, Kevin Jr., Cory, Jesse, Bryan Jr., and Amanda, that I came to realize what the word "love" really means and what a wonderful feeling it is to share such a marvelous thing with my family and my fellow man. Even to this day, I am amazed that it took nothing more than several small, innocent children to save me by teaching me, their Papa, to love.

I have had the opportunity to work with several publishers around the world, but never have I dealt with a group of people in publishing who are as kind, considerate, and honest as the folks at Health Communications, Inc. I am absolutely amazed by how the people in this company stick together like family, coming from many different directions to accomplish one goal, even when it appears to be impossible. Yet, in the end, the game is won and another trophy is placed on the mantel. A heartfelt thanks goes out to Peter Vegso, Tom Sand, Craig Jarvie, Carol Rosenberg, Allison Janse, Pat Holdsworth, Kim Weiss, Kelly Maragni, Sean Geary, Lori Golden, Larissa Hise Henoch, Mike Briggs, Lawna Oldfield, Andrea Brower, Dawn Grove, Jose Garcia, Terry York, Patricia McConnell, Christine Zambrano, Jaron Hunter, Veronica Blake, Candace Johnson, Tonya Woodworth, and all the other team players for their hours of hard work to make this book possible.

Then, there are those I met along the way, those who lived under bridges and overpasses who took the time to feed a young boy who was on the run yet again, a boy who had no one to love him and no safe place to retreat. These were strangers who had barely enough to feed themselves, yet they shared with me. It is that kindness I remember—a kindness that I pay forward to this day with others less fortunate than me. It was not the food or the coffee or the dirty blanket they shared with me, but the simple act of sharing that meant the world to me. Without knowing it, they each gave me a pebble that would someday help me build the mountain of life I yet had to climb.

There is no way that I could complete this acknowledgment without mentioning Gene and Lynn Usher, Peggy Hendrix, Garland Williams, Lloyd Nevis, Sharen Jackson, Bryan and Penny Muckenfuss, Ann Conklin, and my very good friend Terry Persse.

Thank you, everyone.

Let Me Introduce Myself

My name is Roger Dean Kiser. This is my story, but I write it to honor of all of the White House Boys and the abuses we suffered at the hands of our tormentors, our "caretakers."

At the age of five, I was sent to an orphanage in Lakeland, Florida, and I became a ward of the state. "The State of Florida is now your mother and father," the judge had said, shaking his head at the tall, thin female caseworker standing beside me.

How did I become a ward of the state? Well, six months earlier, my mother had abandoned my half-sister Linda, a two-week-old baby boy, and me at our home in California. She had run off with some man, I guess for "a better life."

We were alone for four days. When the police finally arrived, they found me sitting in the living room, holding a dead baby in my arms, trying to feed it cornflakes in order to bring it back to life. They tracked down my mother's most recent husband—Linda's father and my stepfather—and he took Linda and me to Lakeland, Florida, and handed us over to his parents.

But I wasn't their grandchild, and they never let me forget it. Barely a day went by that I wasn't mistreated in some manner. On more than one occasion, my "grandma" would say, within earshot, "We need to put this stupid little bastard in the center for retarded children."

The teachers from the school across the way took pity on me and were constantly threatening to call the police on my grandparents. Then, one day, they carried out that threat.

I had crossed the street on my own to play on the merry-go-round in the schoolyard when grandma came running toward me with a leather strap. She was shouting at me and cracking that strap like a whip.

One of the teachers ran toward her and cried, "Jesus Christ, you are going to kill that boy!"

I was so scared that I messed on myself. My grandma shooed the teacher away, grabbed me by the ear, and dragged me to the back of the house. When they saw that I had messed on myself, my grandfather rubbed the crap in my face to shame me for what I had done. Bawling and howling, I was taken out on the pickle porch and hosed down.

When the police finally arrived, they found me standing in the backyard, buck naked, my arms stretched upward holding my pants to the sun so they would dry.

And that's when I became a ward of the state. I began at one orphanage, then was transferred to another, the Children's Home Society, in Jacksonville, Florida. That's where I became Matron Mother Winters's "boy." This insane, demented woman used me for her private sexual amusement.

I think it's needless to say, but beatings were handed out regularly at that orphanage for the slightest offense. If not beaten, then we got locked in a dark, scary closet when we misbehaved.

It's no wonder that I escaped from that place whenever I could. I would live on the streets for days at a time, but sometimes only for a few hours, until they found me again. I did other "bad" things too, like going to the bathroom or getting a drink of water without asking permission, climbing trees, riding a bicycle, and sometimes I even acted like a child. Once, I admit, I stole a candy bar.

After breaking too many of the rules, I was sent to the Florida Industrial School for Boys at Marianna, along with one of the other boys from the orphanage.

The thought of going to a reform school was very scary, but I couldn't imagine anything worse than the orphanage. Those painful experiences at the orphanage and on the streets could fill a half dozen books on their own. But that's for another time.

As I relate to you the story of my years at the Florida Industrial School for Boys, the particular incidences are still very clear in my mind like nightmares that won't go away, even after fifty years. Even so, the dates and times are not as clear as they could be. I don't even know exactly how old I was when I was there. Even the state didn't know how old I was, having assigned me the wrong birth date, which I discovered years later when I finally tracked down my birth certificate.

When a person has been locked away in one form or another, the days, weeks, months, and years all run together. Most every day, every week, every year is identical to the next. In fact, I spent two terms at the Florida Industrial School for Boys. Both times I was there pretty much just run into each other. I can't say for sure from memory when I left or when I went back.

I suppose the best way to describe it would be like this: Your parents drop you off at the first grade and don't come back for you. You never leave the building. All you know is the way to the bathroom, the cafeteria, and the classroom. Things change, you grow bigger, and the "caretakers" change, but you don't know exactly when. It just happened.

"Exactly when did that occur?" someone asks you. How do you answer that question? You search your memory bank, but it's all scrambled. The only thing you can do is take a guess based on simple logic—like *What song was playing on the radio when I was dragged out of my cottage?* It is this state of childhood confusion, along with a lack of celebratory milestones to go by, that clouds my recollections of the past.

It is bad enough to be a scared, lonely child. But even worse than that is becoming an adult with that same scared, lonely child still living inside. It is that feeling that inspired me to try to make a difference in the lives of children today by sharing my awful experiences, but also by sharing my triumphs despite those experiences.

Often, to some, foster children who are troubled and unhappy seem more trouble than they're worth. *Why don't they openly appreciate the opportunity to come into a loving home? What difference can I make now, now that this child is already broken?*

Know that it is difficult for abused children to trust anyone. Sometimes the miracle to be achieved is not in trying to save the child by turning him or her into a "normal," happy, carefree child today, but instead, looking into the future at the person that child will someday become. It's about hanging in there with unconditional love and giving that child a chance to see what it means to be a good adult. That child will more likely grow into a kind adult and a good parent and grandparent. That is what is most important to teach a child who doesn't know what it means to be a child. The prize is never won at the start of any game; it is achieved at the end of the game. And that can only be accomplished and proven by those who truly love someone. Fortunately, there were a few people in my early life who touched my heart just enough so that I could eventually release the haunting memories of my childhood.

So, not only do I write this book to expose the abuse we boys suffered, I also write this book in hopes that those who have been abused will see that no matter how difficult the task, no matter how bad the abuse, there is still a wonderful faint light always burning at the end of the tunnel. That light is you—standing there waiting for you to hug yourself. It is then that you can begin to save your marriage, your children, and your grandchildren. That is the reward you will receive for having survived the train wreck.

How wonderful it is to stand proud and know that your children and grandchildren will never have to suffer the slings and arrows of the abuse you suffered. There is no greater prize to be had. Yes, it may be a long hard battle, but in the end they will not beat you. You will know that YOU WON, and for that you will stand proud and smile, for you will be the winner of the game. As I am.

Looking Back and Moving Forward

The White House, 2008.

Generally, I'm a little nervous when I am about to give a speech. Even when speaking to groups of children about child-abuse issues, this unusual nervousness comes over me, a sort of stage fright. But this time, for some reason, things were different. I felt different.

I stood silently behind the wooden podium wondering what to say. Slowly, I raised my head and stared at the crowd of thirty or forty guards, each dressed in Department of Juvenile Justice uniforms, numerous Florida State employees, and a bunch of fancy-dressed individuals from the governor of Florida's office, each waiting to hear what this uneducated dimwit had to say.

The word "masturbation" kept coming to mind, along with my memory of the traumatic experiences I had suffered as a small child, even before I had arrived at the Florida Industrial School for Boys, at the hands of the orphanage matron. I thought "masturbation" would be a good word to share with this audience, and so that's what I did. No sooner had that word come from my lips when I saw one of the governor's people drop his coffee cup. Most expressions were of shock, but I saw a couple of the female guards throw me a wink and a smile. Of course they wouldn't have done that if they understood the significance.

I explained to the group that the molestation I had suffered at the orphanage had become a way of life for me, but it was a life I was glad to be leaving behind when I was sentenced to the Florida Industrial School for Boys. I naively thought better days were ahead. I'd been beaten at the orphanage, but it didn't prepare me for the brutal beatings to come. After my first visit to the White House, the State of Florida had convinced me that helping Matron Mother Winters masturbate herself was the lesser of two evils.

It felt strange knowing that the "White House Torture Chamber" stood less than three feet behind me. As I recounted the horrors, rapes, beatings, and alleged killings that had taken place in that building, I kept pointing over my right shoulder with my thumb. I didn't turn away; it was necessary for me not to lose track of any of the faces or the expressions on them before me. I had a very important point to make, and this was the chance I had waited for, for almost twenty years. I was there to have my say, as were four of the other "White House Boys."

When we finished our speeches, the guards and other attendees were led through the doorway and into the narrow hallway of the chamber—still dark, damp, and smelly. Many of the guards covered their mouths; I heard others say, "Oh, my God!"

I suppose the blood stains on the walls and floor were more than a decent civil human being could take. I found some solace knowing that a new generation of juvenile guards found this building repulsive and totally disgraceful.

Afterward, a plaque was presented that signified the official sealing of the White House at the old Florida Industrial School for Boys in Marianna, Florida, and a tree was planted to forever mark the spot where the atrocities had occurred. Then, the crowd headed to the administration building for cold drinks and finger food. As the press began their interviews, I snuck out the side door and made my way back to the White House.

Now, all alone, the White House Torture Chamber standing before me, I began taking photographs. Every two steps forward, the camera lens would snap and a horrible memory from the past was preserved for future generations.

It was very difficult for me to keep the scared little boy inside me separated from the grown man now holding the digital camera. When I reached one of the small dungeon-type cells where I had been beaten, I reached out with a shaking hand and touched the cold, hard wall. Chills ran through my body, and I quickly removed my hand. I looked at the wall I had tried to climb while being beaten, almost to death.

Where are all the puddles of blood that were draining from my body and running down the wall that day? I thought.

Lowering my camera, I looked up at the ceiling. Then, carefully, without thinking, I slowly sat down on the edge of the steel bed, but it was no longer there. I managed to catch myself against the wall before I fell on the filthy floor.

Next, I walked into another small room, the room with a dirty, broken toilet. I wondered if any boy had ever been allowed to use that commode before having "the pure living shit beat out of him." I also wondered why the black boys, who I had heard were beaten even worse than the white boys, called this building the "ice-cream parlor."

Finally, I walked out the front door. I turned to look down the dark, stained hallway one last time. I stood there thinking about which part was the worst of all. Was it the atrocious beatings? Or was it the fact they made me feel like I was a worthless piece of shit? I think I got over the beatings, but I don't think I ever got over that feeling.

Toward the end of the day, we White House Boys along with the present warden of the school (a woman), several guards, and other employees traveled to the gravesite believed to house the bodies of some of the boys who died while incarcerated in the facility. We took pictures and said a few silent prayers, until the silence was broken by the warden's shouts of pain.

The White House Boys were the first to arrive at her side. She had stepped into a bed of fire ants, and her shoes and legs were covered with the attacking insects. In extreme pain, yet holding her composure, she begged for assistance with her eyes. Quickly, three of us White House Boys grabbed the warden, removed her shoes, and rubbed the fire ants off her legs. Within minutes, all was back to normal. The White House boys had rescued the warden.

Who would have ever thought that it would be us—the boys who had been brutally beaten and tortured fifty years earlier—who would save the warden of the very facility where we'd been made to feel worthless?

The White House Torture Chamber was officially sealed by the Florida Department of Juvenile Justice on October 21, 2008.

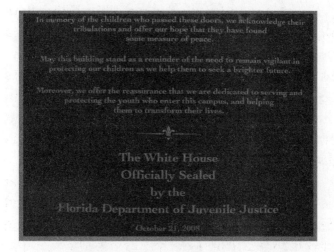

"In memory of the children who passed these doors, we acknowledge their tribulations and offer our hope that they have found some measure of peace.

May this building stand as a reminder of the need to remain vigilant in protecting our children as we help them to seek a brighter future.

Moreover, we offer the reassurance that we are dedicated to serving and protecting the youth who enter this campus, and helping them to transform their lives."

The White House
Officially Sealed by the Florida Department
of Juvenile Justice October 21, 2008

Photo by R. Kiser

White House main entrance, 2008.

Photo by R. Kiser

White House side entrance (the "beating entrance"), 2008.

Photo by R. Kiser

White House hallway, 2008.

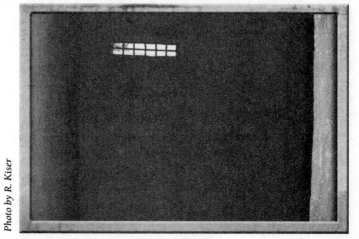

Photo by R. Kiser

White House beating chamber 1, 2008.

White House beating chamber 1 (side angle), 2008.

White House beating chamber 2. The light you see is from the flash and small window; otherwise, it is very dark in there.

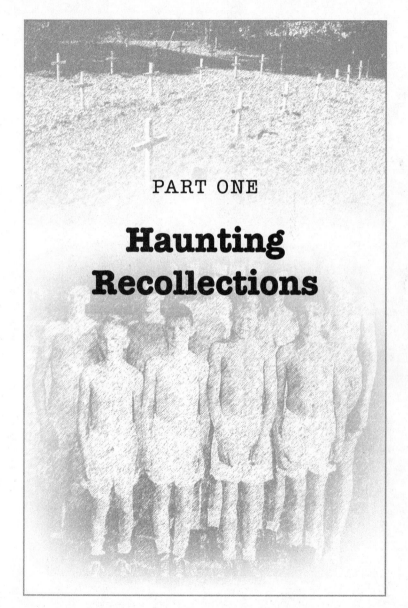

PART ONE

Haunting
Recollections

My Crime Against Society

I had been sentenced to the Florida Industrial School for Boys in Marianna, Florida, by Judge Marion Gooding of the Duval County Juvenile Court for being an "incorrigible child" and "unable to follow instruction." What was my crime against society? I had attempted to run away, once again, from the Children's Home Society Orphanage in Jacksonville, Florida—but other than climbing through an open window in the Spring Park School building searching for food, climbing a tree at the orphanage, taking a bicycle from the girls' dormitory for a ride, and going to the bathroom without asking permission, I had never caused any real trouble. Sure I could be a bit of a hellion at times, but only to protect myself. My true crime, my real "crime," was not having parents to care for me.

That is the real truth of it all.

"You damn orphan kids are nothing more to me than a herd of caribou," said Judge Gooding, before sentencing me and my friend David to the reform school.

I remember that day as if it were yesterday. I recall the hollow sounds of the courtroom doors, the fed-up look in the judge's eyes, and the harsh tone of his voice as he shook his head back and forth in disgust.

I was numb as I stood there before him, being just a young boy looking up at a great big man sitting behind a great big table. I did not know what to do, say, or think. I guess that's because it really did not matter to me anymore. I suppose it was because I had already given up on life. Or maybe it was because there was no one there to tell me what to say, do, or think.

I couldn't possibly imagine that my life could get any worse than it was. I found it unbelievable that anyone on the face of this earth could beat or mistreat children as badly as they had at the orphanage. But boy, was I wrong on that call.

The White House Horror

I hadn't been at the Florida Industrial School for Boys for very long when they called me to the head office. They told me that I would be visiting the White House—a torture room for boys who broke one of the many rules.

When I heard this, I was overcome by heart-pounding fear. I nearly passed out and trembled so badly that my legs collapsed. I fell to the floor and just lay there. The men told me to "get my sorry butt up" and sit down on the wooden bench outside the office.

I shook as I waited there for the two men—six-foot-tall Mr. Hatton and one-armed Mr. Tidwell—who would take me to the White House. I knew the routine well, since I'd heard about it from many of the other boys who had been taken there.

After a wait of about thirty minutes, the two men

came to get me. They grabbed me by my arms and lifted me off the bench. There were several other boys in the office (boys were always coming and going), so I had to try to act as though I was not scared, but they knew.

The two men walked with me across the grass circle that divided the offices from the White House. We continued toward the dining hall. As we rounded the building, I could see it right in front of me: THE WHITE HOUSE.

My mind went crazy with fear. I was so scared, I could not think straight. Words were coming from my mouth before my mind could think of what it was I was attempting to say. I was trying to decide if I should run and hide or maybe kill myself. Anything was better than what was going to happen in there.

When we reached the door, one of the men took out his keys and stuck one into the lock. I looked back over my shoulder, and I saw about fifty boys near the dining hall. They stared in silence. As the door opened, an ungodly odor filled my nose, and I could hardly breathe. I remember trying to step through the doorway, but the odor was so overwhelming that I fell in the short hallway inside. One of the men grabbed me by the back of the shirt collar and jerked it up around my neck, choking me.

One of the buttons popped off my shirt and hit the floor, rolling very slowly around the corner. Almost everything was happening in slow motion. My whole body was numb, and it was very difficult to breathe. I tried to pull the shirt down from around my neck, but the man jerked it once again and hit me on the top of the head with his knuckles. I hit the floor again and bloodied my nose from the impact. At that point, I was not walking at all; my legs would not work.

The two men picked me up and carried me into a small room, which had nothing in it except a bunk bed and a pillow without a case. They put me down on the floor and ordered me to lie on the bed facing the wall. Crying, I pulled myself up onto the edge of the bed and wiped the blood from my nose onto my shirtsleeve. When I looked up at the men's faces, they were plain, cold, and hard. They had no expression whatsoever. I did what they told me to do. What choice did I have?

One of them told me to move my hands to the top

of the bunk bed and grab the bar at the headboard. I did so as quickly as I could. Not one sound could be heard. I felt one of the men reach under the pillow and slowly pull something out. I turned over quickly and looked at the one who was standing near me. He had a large leather strap in his hand.

"Turn your damn head back toward the wall!" he yelled.

I knew what was going to happen, and it was going to be very bad. I had been told what to expect by some of the boys who had been there. (Mind you, some who had been there couldn't tell us what it was like since they were never seen again.) I had also heard that this infamous giant strap was made of two pieces of leather with a piece of sheet metal sewn in between the halves.

Again, everything was dead silent. I remember tightening my buttocks as much as I could. Then I waited and waited, and waited. I remember hearing someone taking a deep breath, then a footstep. I turned over very quickly and looked at the man with the leather strap. There was an ungodly expression on his face, and I knew he was going to beat me to death. I will never forget that look for as long as I live.

I tried to jump off the bed, but I was knocked backward when the leather strap hit me on the side of the face. Blood squirted everywhere—all over the walls, bed, pillow, and floor. The men grabbed me and pinned me to the floor. I was yelling to God to save me, begging for someone, anyone, to help.

"Please forgive me! Please forgive me!" I shouted at the top of my lungs. "Please forgive me! Dear God, please help me!"

But it didn't do any good. God didn't hear me that day. Maybe He was smart enough not to ever enter the White House, even to save a child.

After about five minutes of begging, pleading, and crying, I was told to get back on the bed and grab the top rail again. They warned that if I tried to get off the bed, the whole thing would start all over. I slowly pulled myself up off the floor and got back onto the bed. Again, I grabbed the rail and waited. Everything became quiet, except for the two men breathing really hard. Once again, I tightened up my buttocks and waited.

"You get up again, and I'll make goddamn sure you make it to the graveyard today," warned one of the men, Mr. Hatton.

Tightening every single muscle in my small body, I waited. Then all of a sudden, it happened. I thought my head would explode. The thing came down on me over and over. I screamed and kicked and yelled as much as I could, but it did no good. He just kept beating me over and over. However, I never let go of that bed rail. Then there was nothing.

The next thing I remember, I was sitting very gingerly on another wooden bench in Mr. Hatton's office. The other boys in the office could barely look at me, like somehow they might "catch" my pain. I remember wiping the slobber and blood from my mouth. My body felt like it was on fire. I got up and found that I could hardly stand. *God, God, God, it hurt so badly.*

One of the men in the office yelled at me to sit back down. I told him I had to go to the bathroom really bad. He pointed at the doorway to the bathroom and told me to "make it quick." Hobbling toward the bathroom, I mumbled, "One of these days I'm gonna get out of here, and I'm gonna tell what you did to me and the others."

The man pointed his finger at me and said, "Let

me tell you something, mister, talking like that is a good way to wake up dead tomorrow morning. You understand me?"

Shaking my head back and forth, I slowly walked into the bathroom and closed the door. I almost went out of my mind when I saw my reflection in the mirror. I was a bloody monster. There was blood all over my battered face and in my hair and around my mouth. I took my torn shirt off and let it hang from the waistband of my pants. Then I turned around to look in the mirror at my bloody back.

I started to cry, but I covered my mouth with both hands so none of the boys in the office would hear me. I loosened my belt buckle to get my pants down. It was very painful, but the worst was yet to come. Once they were down, I noticed that my legs were all bloody and parts of my skin were black.

I stood over the toilet and tried to urinate, but it just would not come out. I decided to take my underwear down and sit on the toilet until I could go, but the underwear would not come off. It was stuck to my rear end and legs. The cotton material had been beaten into the skin of my buttocks and was caked with blood. I pulled my pants back up and washed my face, mainly because I did not want the other boys to see that I had been crying. My cheek stung and started bleeding again. I was so scared by the pain and my appearance that I could not stop shaking.

Finally, I walked back into the outer office and was told to report to another office building. When I entered that building, I was so bloody that not one person in the office recognized who I was.

I saw Mr. Sealander, my cottage housefather, standing by the doorway. He, of course, knew who I was because he was waiting for me. He took me back to my cottage and called the office to complain. Then he took me to the hospital where the old nurse, Ms. Womack, soaked me in Epsom salts. With tweezers, she and the doctor pulled the underwear from my skin and sutured up my buttocks. Then she petted that big, ugly cat of hers and sent me away.

All that, and I didn't even know what rule I broke.

Much later I found out that I'd been beaten like that because someone reported that I had said "shit" when I slipped on the diving board at the pool. For as long as I live, I will never forget that vicious beating I endured without even knowing why. I will never forget the monster I saw in the mirror that day. I will never forget what adults are capable of doing to a child. I will never forget that the State of Florida was behind what happened to me and to many, many other boys.

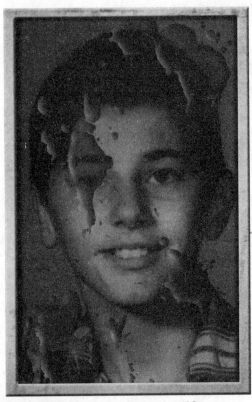

Roger Dean Kiser, approximate age 13

The Tin Box

David and I were friends at the orphanage. We were good friends and shared something that only we knew about, something we would keep a secret for many, many years. It just so happens that David was sent to the reform school the same day I was. As scared as we boys were, it was comforting we had each other, even if it was something we were not going to admit.

The two of us were sent to the main office and sat there for almost an hour, too afraid to speak or even look at each other. I had a lot of time to think just then, and so I thought about the tin box.

It was one night just after dinner at the orphanage when David came running up to me. "I have something to show you," he said.

"What is it?" I asked.

"Can't show you till tonight. Before I do, cross your heart you ain't never gonna tell no one. Never, okay?"

"Okay," I said, crossing my heart.

I waited all the way till bedtime, but David didn't show up. I fell asleep, disappointed that I had crossed my heart for nothing. But then, I found myself being shaken awake.

"Roger, wake up," David whispered.

Groggy, I asked, "What? What's going on?"

"Come on, come with me. I got something important to show you," he said.

Quietly, and on tiptoes, so that we wouldn't wake up anyone, we snuck down the hallway, down the back stairs, and through the telephone room. David unlocked the door very carefully and outside we went.

David led me to the "Christmas Tree," a fifteen-foot pine. He got down on his knees and dug out small tin box that had been buried, not too deep. He pried off the lid and took out the contents of the box.

"Gosh!" I said. "That's only for girls."

"I know, but it's something to do."

David was right. It was something to do, something other than work. We didn't really have any toys at the orphanage, and we spent most of our time doing chores, either inside or outside—raking leaves, cleaning toilets, washing pots and pans . . . "entertaining" Mother Winters. This was something we could do that we might enjoy.

As often as we could, David and I snuck out of the building to dig up that tin box. We'd play with the contents of that box for about an hour. When we were done, David always made me promise I wouldn't tell.

I never did. But there we were at the Florida Industrial School for Boys, and the tin box wasn't ours anymore.

"Okay, you two, follow me over to Dr. Curry's office," said a guard. "You'll get your cottage assignments from him."

We got up and followed the man to a small building. We were told to stand with our noses in the corner, which we did for about ten minutes until we were escorted into Dr. Curry's office together.

Dr. Curry was the head psychologist at the school. He sat behind a large wooden desk and just glared at us with those bulging eyes of his. Every once in a while, he'd puff from his pipe, the smoke curling around his head. He was a heavyset man who wore glasses, and he seemed pretty old, but was probably only about thirty or so.

"You aren't sissy boys, are you?" he asked.

David and I looked at each other. We didn't know why he was asking that question. Neither of us responded.

"Sissy boys? Are you sissies?" he asked again, gruffly.

He leaned forward, picked up a pencil, and pointed it at us. "Have you even worn girl's clothing, like panties or a bra, anything like that?" he asked, raising his eyebrows.

"I, uh, rode a girl's bicycle once," I admitted.

"I won't count that," he replied.

The buzzer sounded on his desk, and he got up. "You boys don't move," he said. "I'll be right back. And when I get back, I want answers."

As soon as Dr. Curry walked into the outer office, I whispered to David, "What about the tin box?"

"You keep your mouth shut about that box," he said, balling up his fist.

"But it's for a girl. If we don't tell, we'll be lying."

"You crossed your heart. You swore. Don't you ever," he said, still shaking his fist.

When Dr. Curry came back, I didn't tell him about the tin box. He didn't ask about the sissy stuff again anyway. He finished interviewing us by asking the strangest questions that I tried to answer as honestly as possible. Then he assigned us to our cottages. I was assigned to Cottage 11, Cleveland cottage. David went to cottage 1.

Ten months later, David ended up "making ace." This meant that he was released from the school for good grades and good behavior and was transferred back to Jacksonville, Florida. Me, I was going to be there for a while yet.

✝

It would be forty years before I saw my friend David again. He'd gone on to become a police officer and later a private investigator. We were in touch for about a year before he was diagnosed with cancer. The day before he died, I sat beside him at the hospital. We both knew he had very little time.

"Remember the tin box at the orphanage?" he asked.

I nodded.

"I wonder if anyone ever found it."

"Don't know," I said, swallowing the lump in my throat.

"I just wonder," he said again.

David died the next day, and with him, my promise to never tell what was inside that box was released.

On those nights when we managed to sneak out, we'd dig up that tin box, pry open the lid, and take out the long, slender, well-worn jump rope with two red plastic handles hidden inside. Then, we boys, well, we'd take turns jumping that rope, hoping nobody would catch us. I wonder what Dr. Curry would have thought of that.

Psychological Help:
My Rehabilitation

"Send in Kiser" blared the speaker on the secretary's desk.

The old woman looked at me over her glasses, motioned her head forward, and pointed her finger at the doorway on my left. I stood up, turned, and waited for the door to open. Dr. Curry leaned out and looked at me with a very stern expression.

"Let's go, mister, move it," he said.

Quickly, I walked into his office and sat in the wooden chair to the left of his large wooden desk. His office smelled like tobacco smoke and already the smell was sickening to me.

I had heard from a few of the other boys that Dr. Curry was weird—and after meeting him that first time for my interview and cottage assignment, there was no doubt in my mind they were right. But no one had the guts to say he was a queer or a pervert, but I didn't really know the difference one way or the other. I had already been molested in one form or another at the orphanage by Matron Mother Winters, Mr. Ball and Mr. Henderson, my orphanage housefathers, as well as a teacher named Bill. So being around weirdos was just a way of life for me.

There was a certain type of sacredness that followed me from the orphanage to this place. It was like a light buzz that immediately began generating in my head and throughout my body when confronted by anyone in authority. The truth be known, to me all adults were nothing more than a bunch of evil no-good bastards. But I sat there, keeping that secret thought to myself.

"Okay," he said in a loud voice, "how many times have you fucked your mother?"

I just sat there in silent fear. The words *Think, Roger. Think, Roger. Think, Roger . . . Think quickly!* began racing through my mind.

"Goddamn it. Are you going to answer me boy?"

"I, I, don't have a mother, Dr. Curry, sir," I stuttered.

"Everyone's got a goddamn mother, boy."

"I came here from the orphanage home."

"Well, you still have a mother. How many times did you fuck her?"

"I ain't seen my mother in a long, long time, Dr. Curry, sir."

He spun his chair around, facing the corner of the wall, with his back toward me. A minute or so passed without a word.

"Dr. Curry, sir. Are you alright?"

"SHUT UP!" he shouted without turning around.

"Yes, sir, Dr. Curry, sir," I said meekly.

"I SAID SHUT UP GODDAMN IT!" he shouted again.

"Are you going to help me be normal one day, Dr. Curry?"

"JESUSFUCKINCHRIST! CAN'T YOU UNDER-STAND PLAIN SIMPLE GODDAMN ENGLISH?!"

"I'm sorry, Dr. Curry, sir."

Without warning, he spun his chair back around. He placed his chin in his hand and stared at me. He said not a word.

"Are you going to help me, Dr. Curry?" I asked again.

He continued to stare at me. There was such a look of hatred in his eyes and on his face that I could tell he hated me as much as Mother Winters did when I would not help her masturbate herself.

Raising his bushy eyebrows curiously, he asked softly, "How many times do you jack off each day?"

I knew what that meant, but I was not going to answer the question. *That's a real private kind of thing and nobody's allowed to know about that 'cept me*, I secretly thought. "I don't know what you mean, Dr. Curry, sir," I said.

His hand slipped from beneath his chin and both his arms slammed down onto his desk.

"You are a lying little bastard."

I sat perfectly still not saying a word, afraid to even swallow the spit that had accumulated in my mouth. My legs began to shake, and I felt my eyes begin to well.

"I want you to show me how you masturbate."

How could anyone ask such a personal thing? How could anyone ask such a nasty kind of thing? I just sat there, afraid to move, speak, think, swallow, or even blink. As confused as I was, I tried to rationalize how this kind of thing was supposed to be helping me. I mean, after all, Dr. Curry was a doctor. He had to know what he was doing. He went to the rich people's school and all. Maybe my doing the masturbation thing was the reason I was so crazy and why I couldn't learn. Maybe I shouldn't do it anymore and then I would be normal like everyone else and no one would ever know about the bad things I had been doing.

Sitting there staring at him, I knew my back was against the wall. I was trapped with no way out. I looked at him closely, searching for some compassion, but there was none to be found. Then, all at once, I became brave. I swallowed the spit that had accumulated in my mouth, and I reached up and wiped the slobber from my chin. I asked again, "Dr. Curry, are you going to help me be normal one day like the other boys?"

His head tilted downward, and he peered at me over the thick rims of his glasses. "You are never going to be normal kid. You are an idiot. Do you hear me? Do you understand that fact?"

"Yes, sir, Dr. Curry."

At that very moment, I feared that I was going to

grow up to be just like the people who were now teaching me, that I would be nothing more than a mean, evil, cruel man. I also decided right then and there that there was no hope for me to ever be happy. No hope.

Photo by R. Kiser

"Dr. Curry's" building, 2008.

The atrocities that occurred in this building will haunt me forever—perhaps even more so than the atrocities that took place in the White House.

Avoiding the Rape Room

I lay in my bed, about two months after being taken to the White House for the first time. I remember seeing Mr. Sealander's shadow on the wall. Several minutes later, the speaker in the cottage fell silent. I drifted off to sleep thinking about the finishing words of "El Paso," which was being sung by Marty Robbins when the radio was turned off.

I am not sure how long I had been asleep when I was shaken awake to see Mr. Hatton and a strange man standing at the foot of my single bunk.

Ordered to get out of bed, I immediately jumped to my feet and stood at attention facing the door leading out into the bathroom. The stranger grabbed me by the arm and said, "I bet this skinny little bastard could really suck a dick." If any of the other boys were awake, they didn't let on.

I had no idea what he meant—or, at least, I had convinced myself I did not know what he meant. My only thought (and horror) was that I was going to be taken back to the White House for another brutal beating. Ordered to move forward, my legs would not respond. Tears began to fall and my body began to shake as if in convulsions. Mr. Hatton grabbed me by the back of my neck and forced me toward the open doorway.

Crying harder now, I placed my hands over my mouth to muffle the sound so the other boys would not think me a coward.

All at once, the strange man kicked me in the backside and said, "Shut up, boy. I'll give you something to cry about in a few minutes, you wimpy little son-of-a-bitch. I bet this skinny little fucker can really suck a dick."

It was then that I remembered what my friend Joseph had told me about several men taking him to a strange place (the rape room we later called it) and then doing it to him in his behind. By then, we had reached the hard dirt area known as the "capture the flag court."

Standing to the right of the court by the station-
ary bars stood Dr. Curry. In a car were two boys and
another man.

"You ever been fucked in the ass, you little
fucker?" said someone from behind me.

That's when I began to scream at the top of my
lungs. I fell to the red clay dirt and began to kick at
the two men as hard as I could. The next thing I
knew, Mr. Sealander was standing next to me,
shouting at the two men.

"I'll call the damn police department!" he yelled.
"You leave that damn boy alone."

A very heated argument ensued for several minutes. When it quieted down, Mr. Sealander sat
down in the dirt beside me and wrapped his arms
around me. Then, he picked me up off the ground
and told me to go into the cottage and take a
shower.

When I entered the cottage, several boys were
standing at the doorway.

"Did they do the bad thing to you?" one whispered.

Unable to speak, I walked to the shower, turned
on the warm water, laid down on the shower floor,
and fell asleep.

The next morning, I awoke in my bed and was ordered to report to Dr. Curry's office.

Dr. Curry made it very clear to me by screaming and pointing his finger in my face that if I ever told anyone about what had happened that I would be buried in the graveyard along with the other boys who had opened their mouths.

Until today—Sunday, September 28, 2008—I have never voiced nor written about this particular incident. That was the second time I had been told by someone at the school that they would kill me if I ever told anyone about what had happened.

That night, if it hadn't been for Mr. Sealander, I know they would have taken me to the rape room. While my memories of Mr. Sealander are mostly good, I can't vouch for his behavior with the other boys. I was fortunate to have found a friend in him. But understand, at a time when friends were few and far between, I wasn't very discriminating.

In all honesty, I don't recall ever being taken down into the rape room. However, on October 21, 2008, at the closing of the White House ceremony, the entrance to the rape room was clear enough in my mind for me to be able to describe it to another fellow.

As I followed the superintendent and media down the stairway into that now-vacant portion of the building, I cringed, afraid that with every step I took, some horrible memory would come flooding back. I was being pushed along by a large crowd of reporters who wanted to see "another room of horror." I walked from room to room, wondering with each step if I might be jumped by a horrible memory. Thankfully, there was nothing.

Steps leading to the rape room, 2008.

A room within the rape room, 2008.

Gee, I Hate to Love Carrots

One day, Mr. Sealander took a group of us boys to the farm where much of our food was grown. I recall how amazed I was to learn that peanuts are grown in the ground, not on trees.

We walked from field to field and eventually came up to a large plot of land where thousands upon thousands of rows of carrots were growing.

I don't know why it came to mind just then, but I started wondering if these were the fields that I had heard about, the fields where some of the "dead boys" were buried.

Rumors were rampant around the school that boys who'd been molested and then beaten to death were taken out into the fields where their bodies would be tilled over and over by the tractors and then plowed under . . . never to be seen again.

I stood there among the rows of carrots wondering if this could possibly be true. I thought about how some boys never returned from a White House beating. *Could I be standing over their bodies right now?*

Mr. Sealander told us to go ahead and reach down to pluck a carrot from the ground. I watched the other boys do as he instructed.

I hesitated a few seconds, but then reached down and pulled up a large carrot. It was covered in dirt, and I pulled my shirttail out to clean it. Wiping off the soil, I looked up at Mr. Sealander. He motioned to me that it was time to move on and that I should hurry up and take a bite.

Slowly, I raised the carrot to my lips. I opened my mouth and crunched down. As I chewed, I began wondering, *Was this carrot actually grown from some part of a dead boy's body?*

I don't recall if I dropped the carrot, but I certainly didn't take another bite, and I never looked at a carrot the same way again.

I Can't Stand to See
Nobody Die

There was hardly a day that went by when one of us boys was not beaten for breaking one of the rules. Having been assigned to hospital duty where I assisted Dr. Wexler and Nurse Womack, I had the unpleasant opportunity to witness the aftereffects of many of the beatings. Boys that we called "pukes"—the ones who tattled on other boys— were always beaten less severely when they broke a rule. Plenty of others, though, were beaten at least as severely as I had been my first time in the White House.

It was usually always the same: first, a soak in Epsom salts, then surgical removal of fibers from the wounds. I did not think a beating could be any worse than my first beating at the White House, but there were plenty of boys who received more licks than I did.

One evening Mr. Sealander instructed me to report to the hospital for evening duty. I thought it was odd because it was later than usual. Shortly after I arrived there, a boy who could not have been more than ten years old was placed on the examination table. He was unconscious or so it seemed, and he looked like he had been mauled by a dog. I assumed he had tried to run away and one of the local farmer's hounds had got to him. I had heard plenty of stories about that happening.

The boy's clothing was torn to pieces in places and blood was everywhere, and he had a deep wound on his throat. Nurse Womack began cutting away his pants and instructed me to remove his brogan boots and socks. After unlacing the first boot, I slipped it off his foot and blood started dripping onto the floor. I suddenly felt very ill and ran from the room to throw up.

"Get back here, you!" Nurse Womack shouted at me, and I obeyed.

I began untying the other lace, swallowing back

my dinner every time it came up. The boy did not move a muscle.

When Dr. Wexler did not show up right away, Nurse Womack instructed me to carry the injured boy to the tub at the far end of the hallway. Another boy was sent in to help me. We carried the boy as gently as a pair of boys could. When he was in the tub, I began splashing cold water on his bloody feet and legs.

The boy groaned and moved, turning over onto his side. Then, he just lay there in the tub in a fetal position. I did not know what more I could do, so I walked out the back door and petted Nurse Womack's cat for a while.

When I finally went back inside, Nurse Womack looked at me. "Get yourself back to the examination room and wait there for the rest of the evening. I'll let you know when you can go back to your cottage."

"Where's Dr. Wexler?" I asked.

"Don't mind yourself with that," she scolded. "Just do as I say."

I started toward the examination room, but glanced back at the boy in the tub. "Is he gonna be okay?" I asked.

"There's nothing more we can do," she said, shooing me out and shutting the door behind us. She walked with me to the examination room. I sat on the table, watching her from the corner of my eye. When she sat down and began to hum, I knew right then and there that the boy no longer needed anyone's help.

"I can't stand to see nobody die," I told her.

"Then put in for a transfer," she replied without looking up.

That I did the very next day, and I was transferred to the dry cleaners.

The Chapel

I guess it is only proper to say that Sunday is a day set aside each week in order to praise God. That was certainly the case at the reform school. Not so much because of the religious aspect, but because I could thank God that Sunday was the only day of the week we boys did not have to worry about getting beaten at the White House.

Every Sunday we were required to put on a white shirt and tie and attend Sunday services at the chapel. The hard wooden pew was not comfortable under normal circumstances, but when one has been beaten, the pew would become even more uncomfortable.

The preacher stood before us talking about the kindness of God and how mankind was his gift to the universe. As he spoke, I looked about the large dimly lit room as Mr. Hatton, Mr. Tidwell, and the housefathers stood almost in every corner. I would quickly look at their mean faces, the faces of men who just the day before had beaten several boys to within an inch of their sanity.

As the preacher talked of love, kindness, and brotherhood, I sat there somewhat in a daze thinking, *How much crap can this fellow spew out?* There was little doubt in my mind that there truly was a God, but I knew, or at least I felt, that he was smart enough to stay away from this hellhole.

My young body jerked and stiffened as the preacher began raising his voice. I watched in amazement as he began flinging his arms around to do his weekly sermon of hellfire and brimstone.

"This preacher is as bad as all the others," I whispered to the boy sitting next to me.

"I know. He smokes cigarettes. I saw him out behind the dining hall one day."

I glanced to my right and saw that Mr. Hatton was looking directly at me. I tried to turn away, but he'd already curled his finger at me to come to him.

Quietly, I stood and tiptoed to the side aisle of the chapel where Hatton was standing. Grabbing me by the arm, he twisted me around.

"You get your little goddamn ass back over to
your seat and stop screwing around. You had best
pay attention. Do you understand me, young man?"
he snarled in a whisper.

"Yes, sir, Mr. Hatton, sir," I whispered back.

As I made my way back to the pew, I began to
wonder if Mr. Hatton's saying the word "goddamn"
in church would make him go to hell one day. As
badly as I hated Mr. Hatton and Mr. Tidwell, I did
not want them to go to hell. I wanted them to go to
heaven so that God himself could beat the holy
goddamn hell out of them just like they did me.
That thought brought a smile to my face, but I
made sure no one saw it.

"Do any of you young men want to come forward
and give your souls to God?" asked the preacher.

I ain't got no soul left to give nobody, I thought to
myself.

Photo by R. Kiser

The chapel, 2008.

This building was the one safe haven on the reform school grounds.

Shower Time

In the morning, when the bugle blew, we boys would jump from our beds and scurry around in every direction trying to prepare for the day as quickly as we humanely could so we wouldn't be late. It was as if someone had turned on the light and thousands of roaches went scampering in every direction.

Within minutes, each of us was dressed and lined up, two abreast, to march to the dining hall for breakfast. After eating in record time, some of us would attend school and others would go to their assigned duties. Every day was hectic and everything and everyone were always moving at a fast pace. The entire system was structured in that manner. This fast pace did not allow time for any of us boys to think on our own, much less consider getting into any mischief.

And, by the end of the day, each boy was so exhausted that taking a fast shower and getting to bed was all that was important.

They say that "a mind is a terrible thing to waste," but the State of Florida had not come to that conclusion. We were not allowed to think for ourselves: we were told when to eat, when to drink, when to shower, when to use the bathroom, what to do, what not to do . . . *Was it ever going to end? Would the day ever come when I would be free to make at least a few decisions on my own? Were the adults right? Was I really too dumb to make decisions myself?*

The showers were timed for each boy. We learned to lather and rinse real fast. But that evening, being the last boy on the list scheduled to take a shower that night, I decided I was going to take a stand. As I sat on my bedside, waiting for my turn to take a shower, I had decided that I would stand in the shower for as long as I wanted, allowing the warm, clean water to run down my face. I would close my eyes to the entire universe and for just a moment in time allow all the fear and terror to drain from my mind.

As my turn came, I walked to the shower room, reached in the stall, and adjusted the water temperature. Placing the towel onto the wet floor, I stepped in the stall, tilted my head backwards, and closed my eyes. Within seconds, I had searched my entire memory bank for a pleasant thought and soon realized that I was wasting my time. There were no memories of girls or cars or friends to be found in such a vacant space.

Placing my hands on the tile wall, I leaned forward and tears began to fall from my eyes.

"BOY!" yelled someone from down the hallway. As I looked through the steam, I saw a man's reflection in the mirror at the end of the toilet stalls. He had a length of a rubber garden hose in his hand. He was swinging it back and forth as he neared my location.

"Why is there a goddamn flood in here, boy?" he shouted.

The water was warm but my teeth chattered. "It was already like this," I tried to explain, too scared to think to turn off the water now.

The water, it seemed, was backing up and running over, and perhaps he'd had that hose with him to drain the excess water. Someone must have reported the flood to the handyman.

I tightened my fists and jaw as he drew back the rubber hose. I stood perfectly still, just like I did for my beatings at the orphanage, and he struck me across the legs. A second blow came, and I stepped backward into the stream of warm water once again, and I closed my eyes. I tilted my head back so the warm, clean, refreshing water would flow across my face as I unwillingly accepted yet another toxic memory into that soiled place in my mind.

"I Earned the Right to Be Afraid!"

As we did every evening, the Cleveland cottage boys marched two abreast toward the dining hall, with Mr. Sealander at the rear of the line. "Move to the left and right and come to a stop," he shouted.

The boys walking to the left of the sidewalk moved out onto the grassy area, the boys on the right moved to the right, and we all came to a halt. Seldom did we move off the path because that was considered breaking the rules, but tonight Mr. Sealander told us to, and we sure did as we were told.

Our heads turned toward the commotion, as a boy was being dragged along by Mr. Hatton and Mr.

Tidwell. From the look of horror on the boy's face, we knew he was headed to the White House.

"Move forward and follow," instructed Mr. Sealander.

Looking about, I noticed from the nervous expressions on the other boys' faces that we were all horrified for the boy, but thankful it wasn't us.

It seemed things had gotten out of hand with the beatings they were giving out these days. They were getting more severe and more frequent. This particular boy, Tony, had simply stepped on his house-father's foot during a game of "capture the flag" to earn his beating.

We stopped at the rear entrance of the dining room. The White House was about 200 yards away. Suddenly, Tony broke free and ran, screaming at the top of us lungs. But within seconds, the guards tackled him and began beating him with their bare fists.

We boys remained quiet as we watched on. We knew better than to open our mouths or even acknowledge that we knew what was happening in the distance.

Mr. Tidwell sat on Tony's chest while Mr. Hatton

unlocked the White House door. Tony screamed, yelled, and kicked as they dragged him through the door.

During dinner, we kept a watch out to see if Tony would somehow miraculously be well enough after the beating to eat dinner. After an hour had passed, we had decided that Tony wasn't going to make it out of the White House.

I kept looking over at Mr. Sealander with that worried look, but he would only smile and wink. "Don't worry about it," he mouthed a couple of times.

As we lined up outside for the return to our cottage, the White House door opened. Mr. Hatton and Mr. Tidwell were dragging Tony out the door by his legs.

I cringed when Tony's head hit the ground as it came through the doorway. As the guards continued dragging him toward us, the boy twisted his body back and forth. Leaves, dirt, and pine straw stuck to his bloody face and clothes. Then, about twenty yards from us, the two men dropped his legs and left him lying in the dirt.

Tony rolled onto his stomach and managed to make it to his knees. We watched on as his housefather, the one he had stepped on, came around the building and stood over Tony. Tears ran down Tony's cheeks, and he cringed in fear.

"You punk ass, little bastard. You're afraid, you little coward!" said the man, as he slapped Tony on the side of his face.

Tony raised his arms into the air. He took a deep breath and yelled as loud as he could, "I EARNED THE RIGHT TO BE AFRAID!"

Again, his housefather slapped him.

In a moment of extreme bravery, one of the boys from my group shouted out, "He earned the right! He earned the right! He earned the right!"

His bravery wore off on us, and we all began to chant, "HE EARNED THE RIGHT! HE EARNED THE RIGHT!"

Mr. Sealander quieted us down as soon as he was able. He assured the other housefather he'd "take care" of us boys for calling out. To us, he said, "You made your point. Let's get moving."

When we neared the cottage, Mr. Sealander lined us up on the clay basketball court and began to speak. I didn't think he'd hurt us, but we were all shifting nervously.

"You boys know that you have violated a serious rule and that severe punishment has to be accommodated. You know that I have to punish you in accord with the rules of this institution. What you did was very serious. As punishment, each of you is to report to the cottage and sit on your bunks for five minutes. I will turn on the radio to measure the time. After you've served your punishment, then you fellows can play basketball for about an hour. Now move it!"

We scrambled inside to sit on our bunks as instructed. All of us felt pride over what we had done. We had a vision of what it meant to accomplish something by standing together—that sometimes "the power" is in the masses, even in the worst of places.

"Was I Funny?"

"Poison Ivyyyyyyyyyyy. Poison Ivyyyyyyyyyyyyy," sang the Coasters from the cottage speaker.

When the song ended, I could not get the lyrics out of my mind. Even the next morning, when we lined up and marched from our cottage to the dining hall, the song was still stuck in my head. Surprising myself, I began to sing out loud.

"Poison Ivyyyyyyyyyyyyy."

It amazed me that I sounded exactly like the singers on the radio. This made everyone in line laugh, especially Mr. Sealander, who was walking at the end of the long line. My friend Joseph laughed pretty hard too.

God, it felt so good inside to make everyone laugh! I had never done anything like that before. There is just something about "the laughing thing" that

makes you feel accepted and like everyone really, really likes you.

I continued to imitate that singing voice on and off for several weeks, which always made everyone who heard it laugh.

Then one day, I was called into Mr. Sealander's study, and he told me to immediately report to Dr. Curry's office. He seemed almost sorry. Dr. Curry didn't like me very much because I would not answer his questions about whether or not I had ever jacked off. I hoped he wouldn't ask today.

I entered the office and sat down on the wooden chair outside of Dr. Curry's door.

He opened his office door and snapped, "Kiser, get your damn ugly little ass in here."

"Yes, sir, Dr. Curry, sir."

I got up and walked as fast as I could into his smoky office. I sat down in a chair, which he had placed directly in front of his large wooden desk. As he sat down, he growled and then spun his chair to face me. He pushed his thick, black-rimmed glasses to the end of his nose and just sat there staring at me. He said not a word for more than a minute.

All at once, he snarled through closed teeth and said, "What's this poison ivy crap you've been singing around the grounds?"

I swallowed and said, "Just a song that I heard on the radio, Dr. Curry, sir."

"And the purpose in that damn shit?" he asked, pointing his pencil at me.

"It makes all the people laugh real hard," I said, feeling scared and intimidated.

"No more of that shit. Do you hear me, young man?"

"What's wrong with laughing, Dr. Curry, sir?"

"I SAID NO MORE OF IT!" he shouted.

"Yes, sir, Dr. Curry, sir." I nodded and looked down at the floor.

"Get back over to your cottage. I'll call Sealander and tell him you're on your way."

I left the office, closed the door behind me, and walked out into the reception area. As I stepped outside, I looked at Dr. Curry's new pink-and-gray Chrysler DeSoto, which he had purchased several weeks before. I remembered the day that he showed off his new car and how everyone who worked at the school was standing around the automobile with him, talking and laughing.

I guess when you're a kid, you can't laugh until you are grown up and on your own, I thought.

I kicked a rock off the sidewalk that flew up and hit his ugly new car on the door. I turned around and looked back at the office to see if anyone was watching. Nothing happened, so I walked back to the cottage. When I returned, I told Mr. Sealander and the boys what Dr. Curry had said and that I was not allowed to make the funny sound anymore.

After dinner, our group marched to the football field for the football championships. Our cottage was in the final playoffs against Washington cottage. We had never made it to the playoffs before, so we were very excited about winning.

At half time, we were down by two touchdowns, but by the fourth quarter, we made up much of the difference. Now Washington cottage was just two points ahead of us. There were only about two minutes left in the game and the ball was within a foot of making another touchdown. I came off the end and positioned myself over the boy who played center position.

When the ball snapped, I jumped over him. With both hands, I slammed down as hard as I could toward the football, knocking it loose from their quarterback's grip. In all the confusion, I just stood there wondering where the ball had landed. Boys were piling up all around me.

"Run! Run!" yelled several boys.

I looked down and saw that the football was in my arms, lying against my stomach. Confused, I took off and ran down the field. I pushed and I pushed, running as hard and as fast as I could, trying to make it to the goalpost. Hundreds upon hundreds of boys were now yelling and shouting at the top of their lungs, as I made my way to the end of the field for the touchdown.

I will never forget the look of pride on Mr. Sealander's face as he patted me on the back for the touchdown that allowed us to win the championship game. Even the men calling the game over the intercom were shouting in excitement about what had happened.

"Do the funny thing you do!" yelled out one of my teammates.

"Make that funny sound!" hollered another.

"Sing poison ivy," Joseph chimed in.

"Poison Ivyyyyyyyyyy. Poison Ivyyyyyyyyyy," I

sang out in my well-practiced high-pitched voice.

The boys laughed and screamed at the sound of my voice coming from the loud speaker as we passed by the table where the announcers sat.

That was a very happy day in my life, a day I will never forget as long as I live. But the following day, that is a day I will also never forget.

I was once again called into Dr. Curry's office. As I entered, I saw Joseph sitting in a corner chair. His cheeks were all wet from crying.

"You don't learn very well do you, Kiser?" Dr. Curry yelled.

"Learn what, Dr. Curry, sir?"

"Did you sing out poison ivy at the ballgame last night? Joseph here says it was him. That he was trying to make people laugh. But I think it was you, Kiser? Was it you?"

He glared at me, waiting for my response.

I looked over at Joseph, who slowly shook his head back and forth, pleading with me to say I hadn't sung the song.

"No, sir, Dr. Curry. You said not to do that anymore."

Dr. Curry reached over and pushed the buzzer on his desk.

"Yes, Dr. Curry," answered the secretary.

"Call Mr. Hatton and tell him to take Joseph to lockup for the night."

He kept his accusing gaze on me.

"Yes, sir."

"Kiser, you go back to your cottage . . . and Joseph, you sit in the other office until Hatton gets here," Dr. Curry sneered.

I should have said it was me. I should not have let Joseph take the fall for it. But I kept my mouth shut. I went back to the cottage and told Mr. Sealander what happened.

"Joseph will stay in lockup for the night. That should be the end of the matter," he assured me.

The next morning, as we rounded the corner on our march to breakfast, we saw Joseph and the guards walking toward the White House.

We stood and watched as they unlocked the door, entered the building, and closed the door behind them. None of us heard a sound as we sat in the dining hall and ate our breakfast. I was so overcome with guilt that I could barely eat.

Fifteen minutes after breakfast, we stood outside and watched as the White House door opened. The two men stepped out, pulling Joseph by his arms. He was backward and his heels dragged on the ground. They continued until they reached the dining hall. When they saw me, they stopped and dropped Joseph on the ground at my feet.

"Here's your damn poison ivy buddy," one of them said, as he pushed the almost unconscious boy with his foot.

I stood there and looked at Joseph, who was unable to move or speak. As they walked away, I looked down into his face.

"Joe, are you all right?" I whispered.

His eyes slowly opened and kind of rolled back in his head. He looked up at me, and with blood coming from his mouth, he said, "Roger Dean, can you kiss me?"

I felt my face flush at the request. "I ain't never kissed no man person before, Joseph," I said.

"I don't mean like that, stupid. Like . . . like someone would kiss you on the top of your head, when they are supposed to like you a lot; sorta like a grandma would do when you're hurt real bad . . . or something."

His voice was quiet, exhausted, and I wasn't sure he would finish. Slowly, I got down on my knees and gently kissed him on the forehead as he closed his eyes. As I stood up, I could see all of the boys, not one making a sound, watching us.

I turned to face the large group of boys who surrounded us, waiting with my head down for someone to holler the words, "Hey, we got us a couple of queers here!" But those words were never spoken.

One at a time, each and every one of the boys, some with eyes red from the tears they were holding back, raised their right hands into the air, pointed their thumbs toward the sky, and gave their sign of approval.

"Did everyone think I was funny, Roger Dean?" Joseph said, as he tried to smile.

"You were funny, Joe. Real funny," I said, as I helped my best friend to his feet.

The Reason I'm Not Smiling, Mr. Hatton, Is Because I Can't

As I quickly walked down the sidewalk to report to Dr. Curry's office as I'd been instructed to once again, I ran into Mr. Hatton. Several days before, I had crossed his path while leaving the dining hall. He grabbed me by the arm and wanted to know why I was not smiling.

"I feel sad inside today, Mr. Hatton, sir," I told him, "and I don't feel like smiling anymore."

He slapped me across the face as hard as he could and ordered me to lie down on the ground face up.

Pointing his finger into my face, he shouted, "Do you want me to take you down to the goddamn White House and beat the goddamn pure living shit out of you, boy?!"

"No, sir, Mr. Hatton, sir. I'm sorry for not smiling when I seen you, Mr. Hatton, sir."

So, this time, as I neared his location, I put on as big a smile on my face as possible, a smile so large, in fact, that my jaw was beginning to hurt.

"You wipe that little shit eat'n grin off your god-damn face before I knock it off. Do you understand me, boy?"

"Yes, sir, Mr. Hatton, sir."

"You get your little ass over to my office, and you have a seat and wait until I get there. You're going down, Kiser."

I stood there shaking, my mind racing in a state of total fear and confusion. *I can't smile, I can't not smile. What then do I do with my face?*

I never did "go down" for that episode. I went to Hatton's office and waited before someone finally told me I could go. I went back to the cottage and waited for someone to come get me. Then I waited in my bed for someone to snatch me up during the night. I waited in terror. This time, it didn't come.

Mr. Hatton's office building, 2008.

Because Mr. Hatton was so unpredictable, this building actually put more fear in me than the White House did. This man almost single-handedly made me afraid to smile, and in fact, I suffered through many failed relationships due to my inability to share a genuine smile with the people I loved.

The Champ

It was the start of boxing season, and word was sent down from the main office that everyone had to report to the gymnasium. We Cleveland cottage boys lined up as instructed and marched to the large building. Within the hour, all the boys from all twelve cottages were seated around a boxing ring, fidgeting in anticipation.

I watched Dr. Wexler and Nurse Womack set up the first-aid station. About twenty minutes later, an announcement was made that the matches would be starting.

Two names were called out. The boys got up and walked to the boxing ring. While they tied on their boxing gloves, the coaches told them some of the basic rules.

The boys entered the ring and faced each other.

DONG! went the bell, signaling them to start boxing.

They charged for each other and began to slug it out as hard as they could. Arms were flying in every direction. Several seconds later, the fight was over.

Out of breath, the boys hugged each other to show that there were no hard feelings, then removed their gloves and climbed through the ropes to take their seat in the stands.

This happened several times, until it was my turn, a turn I wasn't expecting with so many boys in the gymnasium, not to mention the fact that I had never signed up for boxing. Football, yes, boxing no.

When I heard my name over the loudspeaker, my eyes widened.

"I ain't gonna do no boxing," I said, looking over at Mr. Sealander. "I didn't sign up for no boxing."

Mr. Sealander just looked at me and pointed to the boxing ring. And that was enough to get me moving.

I got up from my seat and began walking toward the ring. The hundreds of boys in the stands were shouting and yelling with excitement, but I was shaking and scared. My stomach was churning up my breakfast, and I just knew I was going to throw up, right there in front of everyone.

Please, dear God. Please, don't let me get sick in front of everybody, I prayed.

Once in the ring, the coach on my side said, "No kicking, shoving, or pushing."

I stood there in a daze as he tied on my boxing gloves. The next thing I knew, the bell had rung.

My opponent came rushing toward me as fast as he could. Time seemed to slow down as I watched his gloved fist hit my face with full force, knocking me to the mat.

The referee checked if I was okay. I nodded, and started getting up. I was dazed, but I could see and hear the boys in the gymnasium laughing at me. My face turned bright red. My opponent was laughing too.

That's when I charged at him and started hitting him as hard as I could. I hit him at least twenty or thirty times before he finally fell to the mat. I stood over him, watching his motionless body.

"My God, boy! I ain't never seen no one hit like that!" shouted the coach excitedly. "You must have hit him twenty times for every time that he hit you!"

Still dazed, I looked into the crowd. The boys were hooting and hollering for me now, but I couldn't hear them. Everything was silent.

For the next ten weeks, despite the fact that I didn't want to box, that I hated boxing, I had to take on another opponent. Every week I somehow managed to win the match. Every day of those ten weeks, I felt sick to my stomach and could barely keep my food down. It didn't matter if I was in the ring or not, I was just plain scared.

On the night of the boxing championships, I heard I was going to have to fight a boy named Wayne. Hearing that news almost pushed me over the edge. Wayne was much larger and taller than I was, and he was mean. In the dining hall one day, I had seen him beat another boy with a metal tray without blinking an eye.

I went into Mr. Sealander's office several hours before the fight. I told him I did not feel good and that he should send me to the infirmary to be checked, but Mr. Sealander only sent me back to my bunk to rest.

So, there I was, lying on my bed, listening to the music coming from the speaker. Hot tears were running down my face, and I kept watch on the doorway to make sure none of the other boys would come in and see me crying.

"Roger, time to get ready," said Mr. Sealander, shaking me awake from the brief sleep I'd fallen into.

Next I know, there I am, standing in my corner, watching and waiting for Wayne. When he approached the ring, the coach shouted to me, "Look at him. Look him directly in the eye!"

Slowly, I raised my head and stared directly at my opponent. He looked at me for a second, then turned away, but I kept my eyes on him.

My legs began to shake, my chest began to flutter, and I was about to throw up. Still, when Wayne looked over at me, my line of sight hadn't been broken.

"Now, slap your gloves together," the coach told me. "Show him that 'killer instinct' you have."

"What makes you say I have killer instinct?" I asked the coach, alarmed.

Matron Mother Winters from the orphanage had

said the very same thing about me to the judge.

"This boy has the 'killer instinct,'" she'd said. "He poured ink into the aquarium and killed all the goldfish."

It wasn't true, and the matron knew that. By this time, I learned there was no use in defending myself, that what I had to say meant nothing to anyone, so I said nothing.

I did as the coach said and slapped my gloves together several times, then dropped my hands to my sides.

Meanwhile, in the other corner, Wayne and his coach were arguing. Then, I watched in total surprise and relief as the coach began to untie Wayne's gloves. When the first glove was removed, it was thrown into the ring. The boys in the gym clapped and hollered.

"The Golden Gloves champion is Roger Dean Kiser from Cleveland cottage!" sounded the voice from the loudspeakers.

I fell to my knees, placing my gloves on each side of my face. Then I fell forward onto the mat crying. By no means were they tears of joy. I was crying because I was glad it was finally over. I was tired of feeling sick and being scared. I did not move from that position until the entire gym had been cleared and become silent.

"Come on, champ. Here's your trophy," said Mr. Sealander, grabbing hold of my arm to lift me up.

Slowly, I got to my feet, and I looked around the large arena. I reached down and began to untie the strings on my gloves using my teeth.

"I am very proud of you," he said, and placed his hand on my shoulder. I jerked it away.

Mr. Sealander drove me back to the cottage in his Roadster. It was a small, green English sports car that no boy had ever had the privilege of riding in before.

As we drove, the glow from the streetlights flashed off of the golden trophy, but all that kept replaying in my mind was that troubling statement, "You have the killer instinct."

I slipped the trophy behind the driver's seat. I didn't want to see it, and, in fact, I never did see it again. I wanted no part of something that would make people think I had the "killer instinct."

Death in the Laundry Room

I had been assigned to work in the dry-cleaning department, which was attached to the left side of the laundry building. One afternoon, I was on the right-hand press when I heard a commotion outside on the large cement walkway. Turning to look, I did not see the supervisor, so I walked to the double doorway and peeked outside. Boys were running in every direction.

Not knowing if something was about to blow up, I called out, "What happened?!"

"He's dead, and he's in the tumble dryer!" cried a boy.

At that moment, I saw the supervisor walking toward me, so I ran over to the press and began working on the uniforms.

When he entered the room, I turned to him and asked, "Who's dead?"

"Another one of you little fuckers just bit the dust," he replied.

"What do you mean?"

"Just shut up and get back to work," he snapped.

About ten minutes later he got up from his desk and walked outside as several cars pulled up to the walkway. Lines of boys were marching away, two abreast down the roadway. As the supervisor walked down the ramp, I ran over to the large window and peered outside. Unable to see down the ramp, I went to the door and stuck my head out.

Within ten minutes, the area was completely cleared of boys. Then, several men came out of the laundry building carrying what appeared to be a body covered in a white blanket or sheet. The bundle was thrown into the backseat of one of the cars and fell to the floorboard. The doors were closed and the car sped away.

I ran back to my work station and turned off the steam valves and prepared myself to go back to my cottage. Ten, maybe fifteen minutes later, our supervisor returned and told us to go back to our cottages.

On the way back to the cottage, I heard that the boy who was killed was a black boy; someone else said it was a white boy. (It always confused me why the white boys and black boys were kept separate.)

I heard that the boy, who may have been there to deliver dirty laundry, had got right up into the face of the laundry supervisor and began cursing him. The supervisor told several of the boys to put him in the tumble dryer, and they obeyed. Days later, word was going around that some boys overheard the cottage housefathers saying that the dead boy's body was taken out into the woods and dumped in a shallow grave.

Who would be next? I wondered.

The road leading to the laundry, located near the smoke stack, 2008.

Perhaps I would have been better off keeping my original assignment at the hospital. At least there, they intended to repair the damage, not cause it.

The Movie I Will Never Forget

One Saturday evening, the boys from Cleveland cottage lined up to march over to one of the other cottages to watch a movie. (Saturday mornings were for beatings, but Saturday nights were generally for movie watching. The bad and the good all in one day.)

The large white movie screen was attached to the side of the building and a projector was lined up with it atop the small grassy hill where we sat. Not far from us were five or six large steel garbage cans with steam rolling out of them.

"What's burning in those cans?" I asked one of the boys in front of me.

"It's peanuts," he told me.

"Why would they put peanuts in a garbage can?"

"To cook 'em," he replied.

It sounded strange to me, but right before the movie began, we lined up to receive a scoop of the peanuts on a piece of newspaper for a snack during the show. As the movie was just beginning, the boy next to me accidentally spilled his peanuts into the grass. Unable to clean them off, he left them there to be thrown away after the movie.

Feeling sorry for him, I offered to share my small pile of peanuts with him. As the movie played, I sat with the newspaper lying across my lap. He would reach over and pick up a peanut or two, eat them, and reach for more.

Suddenly, the two of us were being snatched up by the shirt collars.

"What the damn hell are you two queers doing over here?" snarled Mr. Hatton.

"I'm just sharing my peanuts with him," I told him.

"I've been watching you two, and I am trying to figure out who is playing with whose balls over here."

"We ain't doing nothing wrong, Mr. Hatton, sir," I said, my voice shaking.

"You two get your little asses up and stand to the side."

The boy and I got up from our spots and walked to the edge of the building.

"Do you think we're going down?" whispered the boy.

We stood at the edge of the building for almost an hour until the movie ended. We were told to return to our cottages and that we were to report to Mr. Hatton's office the following Saturday morning, a week later. Since it was Saturday night, the scheduled beatings had already concluded for the previous week's violations.

For the next six days, I could not eat or drink anything without throwing up. Almost every night I lay in my bed, covering my face with the scratchy, wool army blanket so the other boys in the cottage would not see me crying.

When Saturday arrived, I walked to Mr. Hatton's office and stood in line with the other boys who were scheduled to be beaten. As we marched toward the White House, I counted the boys lined up in front of me. I was too afraid to turn my head and count the ones behind me.

After arriving at the house of horror, Mr. Hatton took out his keys and opened the side door of the building. Mr. Tidwell looked on. When the door opened, we marched inside and headed down the short hallway leading into the beating chambers. As always, the smell was almost unbearable, and there was blood on the walls, floor, and ceiling.

Reaching the end of the hallway, we took a left and were ordered to stop. There was a small cement cell on the right and another cell on the left. Two boys were pushed into the room on the left and the others were made to stand in the small hallway.

"KISER!" yelled Mr. Hatton.

"Yes, sir, Mr. Hatton, sir," I responded, as I did my best to squeeze between the other boys in order to make my way to the front of the line. He reached out and grabbed the boy behind me and pushed him into the small cell on the right.

"Get on that goddamn bed, grab that bedrail, and I had best not hear a peep!" he shouted.

Shaking and crying, the young boy lay down on the bed and grabbed the rail. I watched as Mr. Hatton reached beneath the pillow and pulled out the leather strap.

I near went crazy as I watched Mr. Hatton bend both his knees and, with all his might, swing the leather whip down upon the boy. The sounds and the screams were like nothing I had ever heard before or would ever hear again, even in the worst of horror movies.

With my mind in a state of chaos and total confusion, I stuck my left hand in my mouth and bit down so hard that blood squirted out. (The scar that resulted still remains even to this day, fifty years later.) I do not remember how many licks the boy received, but the beating went on for about ten minutes.

As the boy slid off the bed and tried to get to his feet, Mr. Hatton grabbed me by the neck and pushed me into the room, knocking the boy he had just beaten to the floor.

"So, we like feeling other boy's balls do we?" asked Mr. Hatton.

"I wasn't doing anything like that, Mr. Hatton, sir. Really I didn't."

"Then you admit he was feeling you?"

"No, sir, Mr. Hatton, sir. We weren't doing anything 'cept eating peanuts, Mr. Hatton, sir."

"Just a bunch of goddamn niggers and fuckin' queers is all they send us nowadays," he replied, pushing me back out into the hallway.

After another boy had been beaten, I was called forward and questioned about the peanut incident. Then another boy was beaten, and I was questioned again. This happened over and over. Each time I was called forward, I feared it was my turn for a beating. Each time, I would be questioned and then pushed back out into the hallway to wait. When the last boy had been whipped, I knew it was the end of the line for me. With my head down, I walked forward and stood before Mr. Hatton.

"I'm sorry for what I done, Mr. Hatton, sir," I mumbled.

"I'm too tired to beat your goddamn queer little ass today. You report to my office next Saturday morning."

"Yes sir, Mr. Hatton, sir. THANK YOU, MR. HATTON, SIR!" I shouted, then ran out the doorway as fast as I could back to the safety of my cottage.

The Fear, the Anger, the Acceptance

"You look at me cross-eyed one more time, and I'll have Hatton beat the pure living shit out of you," said Dr. Curry in a very firm voice.

I didn't think I was looking cross-eyed, but I tried my hardest not to look cross-eyed anyway. Let there be no doubt that when Dr. Curry spoke—or anyone in authority at the school, for that matter—even God himself was to pay attention. If not, God would surely share in their wrath.

"I'm sorry, Dr. Curry, sir. I was just playing around in my mind," I told him.

I watched Dr. Curry as he puffed on his pipe. By now, I was used to the smell of that cherry blend of tobacco he was so fond of. (To this day, the smell of cherry tobacco nauseates me because of the disturbing feelings it conjures up.)

As I sat motionless, as did I on most occasions when visiting his office, saliva began to build up in my mouth. I was afraid to swallow for fear that he might hear me as the slick, wet moist mixture fell down into my throat. The more I thought about the spit, the more I felt my mouth fill up with it. I knew that I had to swallow or I might choke. So, with one big, brave swallow, I allowed the large ball of wetness to slip into my throat. *GULP.*

"Are you mocking me boy?" he asked without looking up from his paperwork.

"No, sir, Dr. Curry, sir. I was just swallowing my spit."

"Did I tell you that you could spit?"

"No, sir, Dr. Curry, sir."

I hate him worse than Mother Winters, I thought to myself.

Dr. Curry began humming some unrecognizable tune. "Hmmm . . . mmm . . . hmmm . . . mmm."

I was afraid to look at him cross-eyed and I was afraid to swallow, so I tried to sit perfectly still, and stared straight ahead. I knew that at any moment this devil had the power to have me beaten and possibly killed, and I didn't want to die no time soon.

"How many times do you play with yourself each day?"

How many more times would he ask me the same damn question? How many more times would I have to say, "Dr. Curry, I ain't never done that kind of thing"?

I denied it again.

"Roger Dean Kiser, you are one little lying bastard. Everyone of you boys do that. RIGHT?" he said, his voice getting louder and angrier.

"I don't know that, Dr. Curry, sir."

"Are you calling me a liar?"

"No, sir, Dr. Curry. I wouldn't ever do that."

The more he talked and the more he hounded me, the more I despised him. *I hope someone kills him one day*, crossed my mind. It frightened me that I thought that, and I hoped that didn't mean I had the "killer instinct."

"You are going to sit in that damn seat until you tell me the truth."

I said not a word and my fists began to tighten. Afraid he might notice, I loosened them and forced my hands to relax. I wanted so much to scream, "I HATE

YOU! I HATE YOU! I HATE YOU!" But I did not dare.

"What's it going to be?"

"I don't know what you mean, Dr. Curry, sir."

"Are you going to sit there all night or are you going to show me how you jack off? Stand up and drop your drawers and let's have a look at the goods."

I knew right then and there that I was as good as dead. I knew that a beating at the White House was now at hand and that there was no way out unless I did exactly what the sick bastard wanted.

Slowly, I rose from my chair and began to unbuckle my belt.

He leaned back, satisfied. "Let's get a move on. I don't have all day."

I wanted to run, but there was nowhere to run. I wanted to hide, but there was nowhere to hide. I wanted to die, but I just didn't know how I could make myself die right there on the spot.

I will never forget the horror of having to drop my pants in his office that day. His eyes scanned my young body as if Santa Clause had just delivered him the perfect gift. He smiled.

As my body began to swell, I watched his bushy

eyebrows twitch up and down and his smile slowly faded. His expression changed and he lowered his head until his chin touched his chest, and he sat there like that for more than a minute. Then, all at once, he jerked his head upward and shouted, "Get your perverted little goddamn ass out of here, you freaky little bastard. DO YOU HEAR ME?!"

I pulled up my pants quickly and darted out of his office in complete and utter shame. I hated the entire world. I knew the day would come when I would get even with grownups. They were all cruel and evil, and somehow I had to save the world from them, even if I had to destroy it.

I can only thank God that a few good, kind people came into my life before I totally destroyed myself because of people like Dr. Robert Curry.

The beatings at the White House were bad enough, but the verbal and sexual abuse were far worse than was any beating. The physical wounds would one day heal, but for some reason, the hatred I felt for Dr. Robert Curry has always remained. It's as if those psychological wounds try to close up, but then something will remind me, like the smell of that cherry tobacco, and the wounds tear open.

Guilty Without a Trial

Though I had taken puffs of discarded cigarette butts at the orphanage from time to time, I was smart enough to know that smoking was not worth a brutal White House beating. Anytime I saw someone with a cigarette or even if a cigarette butt was just lying on the ground, I stayed clear of the area.

This particular day was a sunny Thursday afternoon, and my cottage was assigned to go to the pool for a swim. After changing my clothing and taking a fast rinse in the pump house, I headed out the doorway and began walking toward the pool. Joseph walked around the corner of the building and stopped me. He asked me to wait until he changed into his bathing suit and the two of us would try and get up enough nerve to jump off the high-diving board. He hurried inside.

My stomach dropped when I saw Mr. Tidwell.

"What are you waiting for?" he yelled.

"Waiting for my friend Joe," I responded.

He began walking toward me. As I looked down at the ground, I was horrified to see a cigarette butt about an inch from my foot. Knowing I would be accused of smoking, I covered the butt with my bare foot.

"What are you doing?" he asked.

"I'm doing nothing at all, Mr. Tidwell, sir," I replied.

"Move over to the other side of the sidewalk," he instructed.

I stood there afraid to move for fear he would see the cigarette butt under my foot. I knew if I moved, I was as good as dead.

When he reached me, he pushed me backward with his one hand, and I fell against the brick building. Slowly, he reached down and picked up the small cigarette butt.

Holding it in his outstretched hand, he said, "What's this?"

"It's not mine, Mr. Tidwell. I didn't even see it until you hollered at me."

"Get your little ass inside that building and get your clothing back on."

I turned, walked back into the shower room, and began dressing. Mr. Tidwell sent Joseph out, and then he stood there watching me the entire time. Several times I tried to explain that I had no idea how that cigarette butt got on the ground. But no matter how hard I tried to explain, he would not listen to me.

After dressing, I stood in front of him waiting for instructions. He held the cigarette butt out in front of me and told me to take it. I held out my hand, and he put the butt in my palm. Then he reached into his pocket, took out a book of matches, and struck one with the only hand he had. I'd never seen anyone strike a match with one hand before.

"Might as well smoke the damn thing. You know I'm going to beat your ass when you go down on Saturday, so you might as well give me a damn good reason."

Shaking, I nervously brought the butt to my lips and walked toward the lit match. Within one puff, the cigarette was so short that I could not hold it any longer without being burnt, so I dropped it to the wet floor. Just at that moment, several boys and another instructor walked in.

"Caught this little bastard smoking," stated Mr. Tidwell to the other man.

"No, sir. I wasn't," I replied.

"Walk over there and smell his breath," Mr. Tidwell told him.

The man walked over, placed his nose to my mouth, and asked me to blow.

The man turned and said, "He was smoking alright."

Knowing I was as good as dead and that there was no reason for me to try to explain the circumstances, I just stood there shaking, doing my best to stare a hole in the concrete floor until I was told to report to my cottage housefather.

When I got to Mr. Sealander's office, he asked me to explain what had happened. I told him there was no reason to explain. He asked me if I was guilty of smoking, and I said that I was not. He patted me on the back and told me to go join the capture-the-flag game already in progress on the basketball court.

To me, Mr. Sealander was a kind and gentle man. He knew exactly what I meant when I said that there was no use to try to explain. He knew that the Florida Industrial School for Boys at Marianna had turned into nothing more than a concentration camp for boys, that all sense of right and wrong had totally lost meaning.

On Saturday morning, I walked to Mr. Hatton's office and sat down on the wooden bench. Within thirty minutes, Mr. Hatton, Mr. Tidwell, two other boys, and I made our way to the White House. The five of us walked into the narrow, smelly hallway and made our way to the beating chambers.

As Mr. Tidwell pointed for me to enter the chamber cell on the right, I looked up into his face. His expression did not seem as cold and hard as usual. I smiled and waited to see if his expression would change, but it didn't. For two days, I had hoped and prayed that some form of compassion would come over the man. But, in Marianna, prayers were useless. Even to this day, I ask God for very little.

My heart pounded as I defiantly smoked this cigarette in one of the White House beating chambers, fifty years after that beating. If you are going to be accused of something you did not do, guess you might as well go ahead and do it. This one's for you, Mr. Tidwell.

Bits and Pieces

As I entered the small chamber as Tidwell instructed, I stood at attention. Not surprisingly, the bed was covered in blood, spit, feces, and slobber. I had become accustomed to the site, as had many of the other boys, and we just took it as part of the emotional punishment. Besides, the stains and ungodly smells were the least of our problems when we were in the White House.

I laid down on the bed as ordered, holding my breath, and I turned my head to face the blood-stained wall. I buried my head in the soiled pillow. Suddenly, I felt something cold and hard against my cheek. Slowly and carefully raising my head so that I could see from my left eye, I saw a chunk of tongue and maybe a piece of lip that had been bitten off. Startled and frightened, I jumped from the bed screaming and was immediately knocked backward by Mr. Hatton.

In a state of panic, swinging, screaming, and yelling, I forced my way past Mr. Hatton and made my way to the corner of the cell.

All I could think about was mean old Mr. Ball, my houseparent at the orphanage, cutting off the head of a live possum when I was about eight. With its mouth still moving, he made me pick up the animal's head and roll it down the driveway like a bowling ball. Then he laughed and cut off the tail of the still squirming body, and I screamed. He pushed the tail, still moving grotesquely, into my pants pocket. I will never forget the horrible feeling of the head in my hands and the wiggling tail against my body or the sight of the headless possum on the ground.

When Mr. Hatton and Mr. Tidwell realized what had actually happened—that I had put my face on pieces of tongue or lip—I thought they would never stop laughing. In the hopes of ending the beating, I joined their laughter, still huddled and shaking in the corner.

The beating came anyway.

Can You Laugh for Me?

At the end of a day of work or schooling and before we went to the dining hall, each of us boys from Cottage 11 would grab one of the many sickles or rakes that were lined up against the back of the building to begin the daily ritual of either raking up the pine straw or cutting the grass with the sickles.

This particular day, I was leaning my chin on my hand and the rake handle, gazing out across the grounds. I watched the entertaining antics of the squirrels as they chased one another through the tree branches.

"You had better rake or you won't get no supper," one of my cottage mates said.

I shrugged, dropped my rake, and walked toward the edge of our dormitory boundary. I looked across the way toward the field where some of the boys were gathering for an organized activity. A few of them were goofing around and laughing, but that quickly ended with a reprimand, which I didn't have to hear to understand.

What even makes kids want to laugh? I thought, clutching my fists.

"I'm getting out tomorrow," a familiar voice came from behind.

My heart dropped. I turned to see Joseph standing there. He walked closer to me and placed his hands on top of his head. We stood there silently, watching the boys on the field.

"Where are you going to go?" I finally asked.

"Don't know," he said. Then, as if he really didn't want to think about where he might end up, he added, "We better start raking if we wanna eat tonight."

I nodded in agreement, and we went back to our rakes. I watched Joseph as he worked. He liked to make even lines in the dirt with his rake. I could tell he was not excited about leaving. He had left on other occasions but always ended up back here.

The next morning, I helped him gather his few

belongings before walking him to the cement walk at the edge of our dormitory.

"Can you do me a favor when you get out?" I asked.

He looked at me and waited to hear the favor before responding.

"Can you laugh real loud for me when you get a chance?" I said. "Real loud, like no one will tell you to pipe down?"

"I don't feel like laughin' no more, Roger," he mumbled apologetically.

I watched Joseph as he slowly headed toward the main office. He disappeared through the doorway, and that was the last time I ever saw him.

Over the years I have often thought of Joseph—about the beating he took for me and about the quiet comfort we had with each other. I have never stopped wondering if he was ever able to laugh for me . . . or for himself.

You Are Butter Off Dead

It was at least a quarter mile from our cottage to the dining hall. Three times a day, we lined up and marched to eat our meals. After receiving our meal, we sat down at one of the tables around the large room. At each seat was a six-inch-tall bottle of milk. On top of the milk rested about three-quarters of an inch of cream. We would remove the cream with a utensil, then one of the boys would drink his milk, leaving about one-half inch of milk at the bottom. Next, we'd all place our cream into the near-empty bottle and replace the paper cap. One boy would continuously shake the bottle secretly beneath the table until the cream and milk had been formed into a lump of butter. Then, we'd all spread the butter on our toast or bread.

During this particular meal and butter-churning

process, several adults—three women and two men—stepped into the dining hall doorway. (Of course, anytime a woman was at the facility, every teenage eye in the vicinity went directly to her for a personal inspection. If, by chance, the top of a female breast might be seen, the image was captured in our minds and saved for later use.)

I looked over and noticed that the boy shaking the milk bottle had not noticed the adults or that they were walking toward our table. As they neared us, one of the women let out a terrified scream. "Oh, my God!" she shouted. "He is masturbating."

Mr. Hatton jumped forward. He immediately saw who she meant. As the woman carried on, Mr. Hatton grabbed the boy and jerked him up from his seat at the table. The glass bottle went flying across the room.

Mr. Hatton began beating the boy with his fist about his face and head. Minutes later, the boy was being dragged out of the building. Mr. Hatton, Mr. Tidwell, and three other men were headed for the White House with the boy in tow. The men slapped and kicked him as they dragged him through the dirt and leaves like he was a worthless bag of trash.

The entire dining hall remained completely silent for an extraordinarily long time. Not even the sound of silverware could be heard as almost everyone in the room was afraid to move a muscle. Horror remained in many eyes and on many faces for the entire meal, each boy secretly giving thanks that he was not the one caught making butter beneath the table.

The boy was never seen again.

Photo by R. Kiser

The dining hall, 2008.

The White House stands about 200 yards away from the dining hall. Coming and going from our meals, we were reminded of the severe beatings we endured—or would someday get if we purposely or mistakenly broke one of the rules.

I'm Counting on You

It was time for me to go, to leave the Florida Industrial School for Boys, and, surprisingly, I was in no hurry to leave. Other than the orphanage, this was the only home I had known. And, as bad as this was, it had become my home. The orphanage, for now, was thankfully a distant memory, and I couldn't imagine going back there. But if not there, where?

I had made friends, and everybody knew me as one of the fastest runners who ever came to the reform school. I was one of the best in football, capture the flag, and swimming. It's true that I had to put up with Dr. Curry, Mr. Hatton, and Mr. Tidwell. But here I had Mr. Sealander, the closest thing I'd ever had to a father. And some friends, the closest thing I had ever had to brothers.

Slowly, I walked along, passing cottage after cottage. I stopped, turned around, and looked back toward the laundry where I had worked in the dry cleaning area.

Were they going to send me back to the orphanage? Was Mother Winters going to be glad I was back. I hated Mother Winters. I never wanted to see her again. I didn't want to do those things she made me do to her ever again.

As I entered the door of my cottage, I ran as fast as I could over to Mr. Sealander's office and knocked on the door.

"Come in," he said.

I opened the door, walked in, and stood before him, waiting for him to look up at me.

"Can I stay here with you, Mr. Sealander? Do I have to go back to the orphanage?" I asked.

"Roger, that's not up to me. That is all decided by the court, son," he said.

"Why are they making me go back? The judge said I had to stay here for a long time. That is what he said. I heard him," I told Mr. Sealander, starting to cry.

"Come here and sit down," he said pointing to the chair next to his desk.

"Roger, you're a good boy. You are smart, and you take orders very well. You followed the rules and now they feel you are ready to return to the outside world," he told me.

"But I don't got nowhere to go," I said.

He thumped his pencil on his desk.

"Look here at me," he said, pushing my chin up with his fingers. "I am counting on you. Do you know what that means?"

"Yes, sir, Mr. Sealander. That I'll be a good boy and that I'll do what's right all the time?"

"That's right," he said with a big smile.

"But I won't have nobody to look out after me like you do, Mr. Sealander. Please can't I stay here longer? Please?" I begged.

He just sat staring at me. I had never seen that kind of look on his face before. He looked sort of puzzled and sad.

"Didn't I win the football game for us, Mr. Sealander? Didn't I capture the flag for our team? What we gonna do when I'm gone?" I asked.

Mr. Sealander got up from his seat and walked into his bedroom. "You go outside and sit on the steps, until I call for you," he said.

I got up from my seat and waited outside.

I won't never get no more boiled peanuts and no more movies on Saturday nights, I thought, kicking at the sand.

For about thirty minutes, I shuffled around, waiting for Mr. Sealander to join me.

"Roger Dean," he called to me out the window.

"Yes, sir, Mr. Sealander," I said raising my arm into the air.

"I talked with Dr. Curry. He assures me that they have a place for you to go when you get back to Jacksonville."

He didn't say any more. I could not sleep all night long for fear of what the future might bring. Early the next morning, I shook Mr. Sealander's hand. It took everything I could not to cry. I said goodbye to the boys in my cottage, then I was placed in a car and driven back to the juvenile hall in Jacksonville.

This was the first time I was released from the Florida Industrial School for Boys. I would be back there in short order for another stay. As strange as it sounds, the truth is, I was glad to be returning, despite the impossible rules and the mental and physical abuse. I didn't know any better, and I had no where better to go—thanks to the State of Florida.

I'm All Fixed?

Once again, I was being driven out of the Florida Industrial School for Boys at Marianna, heading back to Jacksonville, Florida. Good behavior and good grades had earned me an early release. I sat motionless in the backseat of the unmarked police car, staring down at the worn tan carpet or at the small tear in the back of the driver's seat. Once in a while, I would shift my eyes carefully upward to look at the fat wrinkled necks of the two officers who were transporting me.

I suppose most individuals being released from a reform school or even a prison would be somewhat excited about being free. Now, at long last, a chance to go back home and be with friends and loved ones. The long dream of having a delicious, juicy cheeseburger, hot steamy french fries, and an ice-cold Coca-Cola would soon be at hand. But more than anything else would be the thought that waiting somewhere in the world were the loving arms of someone who would say the words, "Oh, how I've missed you. Oh, how I love you."

But there was going to be none of these wonderful things for me. I tightened my lips, as my mind raced around in a never-ending circle of confusion. *Am I headed back to the orphanage or the juvenile hall?* was the only thought in my mind.

I was afraid to move my head right or left, as I saw the trees flicker from the corners of my eyes. I had no mother, father, brother, sister, grandfather, grandmother, uncles, aunts, or cousins waiting for me. I knew what those words meant, but they had no personal meaning to me. Therefore, I was not sad at all, just scared and lonely.

"I guess your mom and dad will be glad to see you," said the officer.

I jumped when he spoke, but I said nothing. There was nothing to say.

"Did you hear me, boy?" he asked.

"Yes, sir," I replied.

He laughed, and then hit the steering wheel with his hand.

"What were you in for boy? Did you kill somebody?"

"No, sir. I would never kill anybody."

"Well, you weren't in there for being a priest," he said, and laughed again.

"No, sir. I was there for climbing a tree, riding a girl's bicycle, and for going to the bathroom without asking permission."

Both of the officers broke out in laughter.

"You got one good sense of humor, kid. I can say that."

Little did they know that that was exactly what my crimes had been. It's true the juvenile court judge said it was because I was "an incorrigible child" and that I "would not follow direction." But that's all that I had ever done that was wrong.

I knew nothing about the outside world, and I knew nothing about life, at least about life outside an institution. My years at the Children's Home Society in Jacksonville, Florida, as well as my time at the Florida Industrial School for Boys at Marianna, had taught me nothing. I didn't have any skills, except for how to press uniforms. I didn't even know where money came from or how you get it.

How does one become a policeman or a fireman? Do you just go to the station and ask them to make you a policeman? I had no idea how that process worked.

These are just a few of the thousands of things I didn't know. No one ever took the time to teach us anything about the real world. They just fed us, clothed us, housed us, and educated us in the basic subjects.

Once we arrived in Jacksonville, I was turned over to the juvenile authorities and locked in a small cell, with diamond-shaped wire on the door and windows. For hours, I stood at the window looking at the side of the red-brick building in the alleyway. Hour after hour I stood counting the bricks on the building. First, counting bricks from the right, then from the left, as far as the wire would allow me to see. Then I would count the bricks from up and down, again for as far as the diamond wire would allow me to press my face against the cold steel.

"What am I going to do with you, boy?" the

judge asked when I was finally brought before him.

"Send me to the electric chair," I replied.

"Do you want to go to the electric chair?" he asked, leaning forward in his large black chair.

"No, sir."

"Then why did you say that?"

"I don't know."

I knew exactly why I said that. I just didn't care about anything anymore, not even about myself or what might happen to me. Somehow, going to the electric chair seemed like my only choice.

Things get hazy for me at this point. I went from this home to that home, but I eventually ended up living on the streets of Jacksonville for almost a year.

When I was finally "captured," I was already in my mid-teens, and by juvenile court order, I was enrolled in the United States Army. A year and a half later, I was dishonorably discharged.

I returned to the streets of Jacksonville where I survived for another year or two. At about age nineteen, I was sent to prison for "contributing to the delinquency of minors," for which I received a full pardon a few years ago.

I walked out of prison in 1969. It was the first time in my life I was totally free of the system. From that day forward, and for the next fifty years, other than a few traffic violations, I never again violated or broke the law.

For forty years following, my life had very little meaning. I traveled the United States in search of meaning. I worked hundreds of menial jobs. I was married six times and divorced five times. I never drank or used drugs, but I remained almost totally friendless and was told by many that I was a very kind person but that I was the most unaffectionate person they had ever met.

Finally at age fifty-one, I stopped being afraid. With only a sixth-grade education, I became a writer, an author, and a child advocate.

It is not only sad what I missed from the world, but it is also sad what they missed from me. I had so much to give to a world that had totally forgotten me as a child. I'm giving it now, for the child I was.

The Note

A note is born,
It's crystal clear.
It awaits your words
So that it may hear.

With beer as thought
And drinks as ink,
The note progresses
And begins to think.

It develops its tone,
Based on sight and sound.
The lessons provided
Were never profound.

A belt, a bible,
At worst a sword
The note begins signing
Its awkward chord.

With slobber on sandals
It struggles to breathe.
With braces on eyeballs
Its mind never teethes.

Its crystal, now clouded
Unable to steer.
Rainbows never color
When shining from fear.

From rusted suggestion,
It struggles to call.
Another note locked forever
Out of Carnegie Hall.

—Roger Dean Kiser

PART TWO

The Child Now Speaks as a Man

So, This Is the Fellow

I watched him closely as he approached me. Closer and closer he came toward me. All at once, he came to rest directly in front of me. All I could do at that point was gaze deep into his dark blue eyes.

As I stood there staring at him, I said to myself, "So this is the guy who spent several years in a federal penitentiary."

I was amazed as my eyes slowly studied his face. He did not look like the criminal type. However, his face was somewhat sad and his eyes drooped a bit. I could not help but notice a deep-seated kindness to his facial features. Yet, the corners of his mouth pointed down as if he were a sad circus clown.

I had seen pictures of him throughout the years. Even as a little boy, he had those same expressions.

Several years ago, he finally admitted to me that as a little boy he had been molested for many years. I already knew, of course, but I never said anything to him about it. I had wondered for years when he was going to get around to admitting it to me. I guess that somewhat explains the look of sadness that is always present on his face. Not to mention the look of distrust I see every time I look at him.

I moved my eyes about his face and could tell the sadness I was seeing went much deeper than just the exterior. Slowly, his mouth started to open. I think he wanted to tell me more, but then he closed his mouth and just stood staring at me.

There was a time when that balding head of his was full of rich, dark brown hair. A time when his sagging eyelids were fully erect, soaking up the energy of his youth. A time when he was embarrassed when called "a hero" after pulling five people out of a burning car. Not to mention, the time he saved a cat when four teenagers had ripped off its front leg.

Is this the fellow who went on national television in February 1991 with Tom Brokaw to expose the manufacturing of dangerous ammunition that

killed several Americans during the Gulf War? The
same guy who remained friendless for years for
doing "such an evil thing" to his coworkers at the
Riverbank Army Ammunition Plant in Riverbank,
California?

In spite of all I knew about this fellow and considering all that happened to him in his past, I did
not see any meanness or hatred in his eyes. What I
did see was a never-ending sadness and a blank
stare of depression. I guess loneliness became his
own personal monster. It was a fight he was never
able to conquer. Mix in a whole bunch of loneliness
and a few batches of disappointment, and his bad
dream would never have an end.

Still, in spite of it all, he has been a good friend
to me throughout the years. He has always helped
his friends and his neighbors. Never once did he
ever expect anything in return. Not even a "thank
you" was expected.

He never actually told me so, but I know he is
very proud of the fact that he did not turn out to be
a child abuser himself. I know there were many
times when he did not know what the term "right"
even meant. He was a fellow doing his best to make

sure he did not repeat the mistakes of his own caregivers.

There, before me stood a fellow who had no idea how to be a father. There was not one day in his memory when he could relate to what having a mother and a father was supposed to be like.

I smiled at him as my eyes left his for a second. I reached down and picked up the shaving cream from the bathroom counter. Quickly, I looked back up to see if he was still looking at me. He just stood there, staring at me with the can of shaving cream in his hand. I guess he was waiting for me to make the next move.

"Well, old man! How about let's shave ourselves," I said to my reflection in the mirror.

Childhood Memories

I suppose we all have memories of our youth. The time we went swimming with our friends and screamed at the top of our lungs as we slid down the waterslide. Our first time on water-skis at the lake and feeling the cool wind on our faces. The time we went to see a scary movie, and when it was over, we laughed about it in an attempt to convince our friends that we were not really scared. And what about that first tender kiss in the backseat of a car? Will we ever forget that? Oh, how grown up we felt. And let us not forget the high school football games and all the pep rallies we attended. We shouted and yelled with our friends—what fun times they were! How great it was to ride down the sidewalk on a bicycle in the evening to meet up with friends on their bicycles so we could ride around the neighborhood.

Well, I never did any of those things, not one single one of them. As I look back, I do not miss any of the things most of you experienced as children. But what I do miss is never having had the opportunity to open a refrigerator door and make a sandwich when I was hungry. I miss never having had a cold glass of milk with my food. I miss never having a shirt and a pair of pants that belonged just to me. I miss never having had a picture of a fond memory to hang on my bedroom wall.

But I'm not unhappy, not anymore. My refrigerator has three doors, and there is ice-cold milk for anyone who wants some. My pantry is filled with hundreds of cans of meat, fruit, and vegetables. We'll never go hungry. My closet is full of clothes and shoes, and they all belong to me. And the walls of my home are covered with dozens upon dozens of family photos, and yes, those photos are snapshots of happiness.

Would my life have been different if I had the memories of others? With wonderful memories inside my head, would I still have gone to the reform school, jail, and then on to prison? Exactly what did having none of those memories teach me?

It taught me that I am lucky to have survived and that I should appreciate what is important in life. Tonight, I will stand out on my front porch with a glass of cold milk in hand, and I will give myself a toast. Not because of what I became, but because of what I did not become.

When I Speak to Children

I have been invited speak at many gatherings. I have spoken at Kiwanis and Jaycee conventions, 4-H Clubs, several colleges, and universities, but the speeches I remember most, those that affect me the most, are the speeches I have given to children in the public school system.

As I talk about the realities of child abuse and read my stories to them, I keep my eyes on the crowd and try to decide who is or is not listening. I often become emotional when I read and speak, mainly because I can recognize the children who know exactly what I am talking about. I can see the hurt in their eyes and the pain on their faces.

The children who know do not blink very often, and they stare straight ahead, mouths open. They swallow just before the salvia begins to drip from their lips. They look amazed that someone is able to tell them how they secretly feel, that someone is able to tell them what is hidden in that dark and secret place inside their hearts.

"Can you help me?" is written all over their faces.

I look at each and every one of them, and then I wink with my right eye. They smile, ever so slightly, knowing that I know what's there inside and that I would hug them and make the pain go away if I could.

Generally, after each speech, I am silent while driving back to my home, with their innocent little faces appearing one after another in my mind. Though I ask God for very little, I do ask Him to help those children in pain so that they never know the loneliness I had felt for so many years.

Fostering Kindness

I think it is true that many people are not suited to be foster parents, and why they take on such a responsibility is unclear. However, there are people out there who are good and willing to take a chance on a troubled child. In many cases, by the time foster parents receive a child into their home, the damage to that child has already been done. It can be so extensive that it will take years to turn things around. Salvaging the childhood may already be a lost cause unless the child is very young.

Many people who take in abandoned children hope to make a difference in that child's life, and while it may not seem apparent at the time, they are making a difference, maybe not right now, but hopefully someday something will click and that child will be able to grow into a better adult because of some kindness he or she received from a foster parent.

I remember the first time I was in an actual home, and I don't recall how long I was there, but it wasn't very long, maybe a day. I sat there watching the woman as she read the local paper, wondering why this stranger and her husband would take me into their home. *What was the catch?*

I noticed tears running down her face. "Are you okay?" I asked.

She wiped her eyes with a tissue and looked at me. She told me she had just read an article about four teenagers who were killed in an automobile accident.

"You don't even know them," I said sort of coldly. "I ain't never cried for nobody who died."

She looked directly into my eyes. "You're not such a hardnosed boy," she said. "I can see that by looking at your face. The truth of the matter is that you just don't know how to feel about certain things."

She and I spent the next several hours on her front porch drinking Coca-Colas and talking. She didn't ask a bunch of dumb questions like most adults. I don't remember all that was said, but she talked about the good things in the world and tried to teach me something worthwhile. She tried to make me feel worthwhile. When she hugged me tight, my body went limp. I'd never felt such unconditional love before. She was a stranger, but she'd done more good for me during that talk than anyone had ever done for me up until then.

It is amazing how much money the state spent on unwanted children like me. That woman accomplished more in five hours with a bottle of Coca-Cola than the state did in a dozen or so years.

It is foster parents like her that I hope for the orphans of today.

My Thoughts on Today's Juvenile Guards

In most cases, a guard working in a juvenile detention facility does not hold a high-paying position. Most likely, there will be no family vacations to Paris, France. With luck and smart budgeting, they *might* be able to afford a trip to Disney someday.

Any person who works as a guard in a juvenile facility has a very difficult task. They have much more responsibility than a guard in a prison for adults. It takes a very special person to work with children. That person must not only be a guard, but must also take on the responsibilities of teacher, counselor, and in some cases, trusted friend. A juvenile guard must find a balance between firmness and kindness—always being firm, while at all times, being kind, respectful, and considerate of the children they guard.

In many cases, it is important to remember that the juvenile guard must protect the child from him- or herself more so than from society. The job of being "a guard" is more than just guarding. This job must entail making a difference so that the job of "a guard" will no longer be necessary.

I Hold No Grudges, But One

I do not hold any grudges against the men who beat me. If they had not beaten me, other men would have done the job. Those were the rules. Beat the boys who break them. To them, it was a job they were paid to do. I have always wondered, however, if they were ever the least bit troubled by handing out those brutal beatings for the slightest infraction.

In all honesty, I have to admit that I do hold hard feelings toward the psychologist. His perverted comments and actions combined with the pure hatred that oozed out of him toward me is more than I can stomach, and I do not believe I will ever forgive him. To think of all the children who were at this sick man's mercy for so many years makes me shudder and weep inside.

To My Abusers

Because of the way you treated me as a young boy, I lived much of my life alone. But for some strange reason, you have made me stronger, stronger than most people I know.

The brutality you bestowed upon me as a child has given me a very compassionate heart. I have more compassion in my heart than most people I know.

Because of your thoughtless actions, you have made me wiser, wiser than most. And because of you, I have become an alert adult. You taught me to stay on guard and to never relax. I now live my life more on guard than most other people I know.

You also taught me how to feel unhappy, much more unhappy than most other people I know. For a long time, I did not know how to love, how to laugh, how to smile, how to joke, or how to fool around. But because you taught me how to be unhappy, I am able to recognize how important it is to be happy now that I've learned how. You've also taught me one other thing, the one thing I have up on everyone I know. I can cry way more tears than anyone can imagine.

In Closing

The years of abuse I endured as a child gave me a very clear look at how cruel and inhumane people can be. Instead of the love I should have felt as a boy, I felt fear, a feeling I lived with each and every day of my childhood, a feeling instilled in me by those responsible for my care.

As a little boy at the orphanage, I heard and saw the news that millions of people were being tortured overseas. I heard that people were beaten and shot in the head and some were buried alive. I heard that my country, the United States of America, would put an end to the torture and would save all the people, everywhere in the whole wide entire world.

I did my best to believe those words, but how could they possibly be true? How could such a thing be true when we American children weren't being saved from our own demented caretakers? There comes a time when we, as adults, have to look at what is fact and what is fiction. We must take the time to look deep within our hearts to feel what is true. I know that humankind is not perfect, and I know that mistakes are made by all. But my own country did a horrible disservice to its very own citizens who completely relied on it to take care of them.

For many years, I wanted retribution, but no one would listen. I wanted the atrocities we children suffered to come to light, to be acknowledged, so that we could move on. After years of writing about my experiences and posting them on my website, others who had endured the same tortured youth started to contact me. Hundreds of men have been coming forward, and it is only now that so many voices have joined together to shout, "WE EARNED THE RIGHT TO BE HEARD!" that people in our government will listen and acknowledge us.

Appendices

From the Florida archives

Appendix I. Press Release to the Governor of Florida and the United States Department of Justice Attorney.

********** Press Release **********

Justice Hugo Black once stated:

"The Press was protected so that it could bare the secrets of the government and inform the people. Only a free and unrestrained press can effectively expose deception in government. And paramount among the responsibilities of a free press is the duty to prevent any part of the government from deceiving the people." Hugo L. Black
New York Times V US (Pentagon Paper)

There are certain accomplishments each of us wish to complete during the course of our lives.

There is always a beginning, middle, and hopefully a successful ending.

For the last several months, we have done our utmost to expose the beatings, floggings, rapes and possible murders of as few as 32 and possibly many more children while in the care of the State of Florida in the 1950s and 60s. Few people want to remember, or even care for that matter, that these children's lives meant nothing.

Each one of these was a young child, and each now lies in their forgotten grave, hidden away in the thick underbrush of the North Florida woods. We have pleaded, screamed and cried for these abandoned children and now are demanding to know who they were. We have presented this story on television, radio and it has been published in more than sixty newspapers.

We humbly hope and ask that the Governor of the State of Florida will carry forth our cause and bring justice to these children and bring peace to their families. We know in our hearts that the Governor is the type of man who will fight for what is right and just for these forgotten children. We sincerely believe the Governor and others understand the importance of this matter and that those children lying in those unmarked greaves deserve the same consideration and respect that all children should have.

Our elected officials have a legal responsibility and a moral obligation to correct the injustices these children and others have endured as wards of the State of Florida. We ourselves as victims of the abuse while at the Florida Industrial School for Boys at Marianna beseech the public and the media to demand an accounting and identification for these children, immediately before, once again the underbrush covers their graves and they are again forgotten. It is imperative that those who inflicted the abuse and even caused the death upon innocent children be held accountable for these atrocities.

The White House Boys organization respectfully requests the Governor of the State of Florida and the United States Department of Justice order and conduct a full investigation into the deaths of these children. We sincerely hope and believe the Governor will find a true sense of justice and urgency in ordering that these graves be opened and the identities of these forgotten children finally be revealed and that a proper burial be conducted. In the past history of the State of Florida they have made a concerted effort to identify the remains of early settlers, sunken ships and many remains and bounty pulled from the surrounding shores of Florida; these children deserve no less respect. We implore the Governor not to waste another day in bringing closure to this past travesty and finally make an effort to give peace to all who suffered at the Florida Industrial School for Boys.

Appendix II. Roger Dean Kiser's Speech, October 21, 2008

As I stand here before you today, the White House Torture Chamber less than four feet behind me, it is strange that the only word that comes to my mind is the word "masturbate." Between Matron Mother Winters at the orphanage and Dr. Robert Curry, the psychologist you hired to straighten we boys out, that was the only word I ever heard come from these two individuals' mouths. During the first twelve years of my life that seemed to be the most important thing the State of Florida wanted to know about me. It was bad enough never having had a real mother, but to have to sit through that type of degrading language was scary and disgusting. Governor, I have always wanted to say those words to you.

The term "reform school" is supposed to be a positive place not a negative. You, the State of Florida, became my parents by an order of the court and placed me in a Jacksonville, Florida, orphanage. You, not I, chose to make that decision. I, being only four or five years old, had no choice in the matter. You had a responsibility to teach and prepare me for a life outside the orphanage. For seven years, you are the one who allowed me to sit on the end of my bed with only a single broken roller skate wheel to play with. For seven years, I sat there rocking back and forth on the end of my bed, my mind wasting away while I spun that single roller skate wheel around and around more then one-hundred million times. When I was not spinning that wheel I was over at Mother Winter's room laying naked, my little head on her bare chest while she had me masturbate her.

But because I took one of the girl's bicycles from the dormitory, climbed a tree now and then, and went to the bathroom or got a drink of water without asking permission, you sent me way to this ungodly place. Whatever goodness might have been left of me at the age of twelve; you finally destroyed by beating the pure living hell out of me. You almost killed me. When I exited this damn building I was so bloody that no one could recogniz me. I walked into the bathroom in Mr. Hatton's office and I screamed in horror when I saw nothing more than a bloody monster in the mirror. Shaking and screaming, I begged Matron Mother Winters to please come and save me from you bastards. "I'll help you masturbate Mother Winters, really I will and I won't complain ever again." YOU CAUSED ME TO BEG FOR MY MOLESTER TO COME AND SAVE ME! THAT'S WHAT YOU DID TO ME!

Gentlemen, today, almost fifty years later, I now stand before you and I am still not sure if this building will ever allow me to smile. But that's not the worse of it all. A secret inner hatred of society and a fear of my fellowman will forever be instilled and kept secretly hidden deep inside me because of this

White House building, the Florida Industrial School for Boys at Marianna, Dr. Robert Curry, Mr. Hatton, and Mr. Troy Tidwell.

Was my secretly riding one of the girl's bikes without the orphanage matron's permission, or climbing up a thin tall pine tree, or stealing a candy bar from the Patio restaurant because I was hungry worth the price the State of Florida made me pay?

I was not a murderer, a rapist, or a burglar. I was a danger to no one, other than maybe myself. As a child, I had never hurt anyone, not even under the slightest of terrible circumstances. I was just an innocent, confused, incorrigible, hungry, unwanted, and unloved young boy who needed someone to let him know that he had a value to someone, somewhere in the world.

My entire adult life, those two horrendous beatings at the White House have been very difficult battles to deal with—one moment loving children, animals and most of humanity; the next moment a temper exploding into a fit of rage trying to protect myself from those who probably do not wish to harm me, but I cannot afford to take such a chance ever again.

I stand here today in remembrance of all the boys

who were beaten, raped, and abused by this facility. But one that I will remember the most will be the boy who had his skin whipped off his back in one chunk from his shoulders to his knees.

I don't know how many boys were killed here, and I don't know if that will ever be known. But I do know this: Many a good little boy walked into this damn torture building but a lot more little Charlie Mansons walked back out than did good little boys. You should be ashamed of yourselves.

I can only pray that things have changed for the children of today.

Appendix III. Rumors, Unanswered Questions, and Theories

I suppose in any situation there are rumors flying around from every direction. That is certainly the case here as the United States Department of Justice begins its investigation into the matter. However, having personally witnessed the removal of a body from the laundry room is more than speculation or rumor. Three or four other witnesses have come forward telling of similar incidents during their stay at the facility. Additional stories are beginning to surface about secret books and maps located in the attic of the chapel, books marked "Deaths and Graves."

One ninety-year-old woman claims that her husband, now deceased, brought home several boys from the facility and molested and killed them by driving an ice pick through their heads. Stories of boys having been killed and then plowed under out in the fields of Jackson County are coming in from every direction. A former Army Ranger tells of having seen, on three separate occasions, three bodies being taken out of the White House and that there was very little doubt in his mind the boys were dead. Another account tells of a boy taken to the chamber for a beating who fought back and was beaten so badly while kicking at the guards that part of his testicles were severed from his body by the leather and metal beating strap. I recall at least five boys who simply disappeared during the night or after being taken to the White House for punishment. How many boys went missing from the facility? Who can account for them?

A report that I find strange, but not surprising, is that two weeks after the sealing of the White House Torture Chamber ceremony on October 21, 2008, there was an inch of water covering the floor. The speculation is that the chambers and walls had been pressure-cleaned to get rid of any DNA evidence. It has also been circulated that the original books in which the children signed in have been misplaced and that the new books being presented record the boys' names in all the same handwriting. Could the books have been altered to remove any possibility that anyone could discern which boys had gone missing?

To me, the circumstantial evidence is clear. I have personally received more than six hundred e-mails from people claiming to have been beaten or to have personally witnessed beatings and even killings. I am not the only "White House Boy" to have received such e-mails. It was this never-ending onslaught of letters, telephone calls, and e-mails that caused the White House Boys Organization to contact the office of the Governor of Florida and request a full investigation into the alleged deaths and to answer the question why there are thirty-one graves out in the North Florida woods without any identification or public records regarding their deaths.

Appendix IV. News Article Recounting the Horrors

JUVENILE JUSTICE

Reform school alumni recount severe beatings, rapes

Half a century ago, victims say, vicious beatings and rapes ruled the day at Florida State Reform School.

BY CAROL MARBIN MILLER
cmarbin@MiamiHerald.com

The Florida State Reform School—more dungeon than deliverance for much of its 108-year history—has kept chilling secrets hidden behind red-brick walls and a razor wire fence amid the gently rolling hills of rural North Florida.

Established by state lawmakers in 1897 as a high-minded experiment where "young offenders, separated from the vicious, may receive careful, physical, intellectual and moral training," the reformatory instead became a Dickensian nightmare.

Three years after the facility opened, kids were found chained in irons. A 1914 fire took six young lives while guards "were in town upon some pleasure bent," records say. And in the 1980s, advocates sued to stop the state from shackling and hogtying children there.

On Tuesday, about a half-dozen alumni will return to what is now called the Arthur G. Dozier School for Boys to confront the most painful chapter of their troubled lives.

The White House Boys, as a group of grown men now call themselves—kept one of the institution's most shameful secrets for half a century: what was done to them inside a squat, dark, cinder-block building called The White House.

There, they say, guards beat them ferociously with a lash, some dozens of times. Some men say they also were sexually abused in a crawl space below the dining hall they call the "rape room."

State juvenile justice administrators, who have not denied the allegations, will dedicate a memorial to the suffering of The White House Boys—who found one another through the Internet—at a formal ceremony at the Marianna campus Tuesday.

They number in the hundreds, perhaps even thousands.

REVISITING HISTORY

In recent weeks, in a bid to improve transparency, administrators have lifted the veil of secrecy that surrounded Dozier and programs like it, allowing *The Miami Herald* to review century-old records and tour the remote campus.

Robert Straley, 64, a Clearwater man who sells novelties at city events and music festivals throughout the South, still recalls vividly what happened to him in the white stucco cracker house in March 1963.

The instrument of his torment was a long leather strap—like the kind used in old-fashioned barber shops, except that part of it was made of sheet metal.

"If I had them people in front of me, I'd have to ask them if they realize how many lives they destroyed," Straley said. "They beat you. They put the rage in you."

"When you inflict that much pain and brutality on a child, they're traumatized for life," he said. "Period."

Troy Tidwell, 84, a retired supervisor still in Marianna, acknowledges that children were disciplined at The White House, though he denied any of the inmates were injured.

Originally, Tidwell said, guards "spanked" the boys with a three-inch-wide, 18-inch-long board but traded in the paddle for the strap because "we were afraid the board would injure them."

"Kids that were chronic cases, getting in trouble all the time, running away and what have you, they used that as a last resort," Tidwell said. "We would take them to a little building near the dining room and spank the boys there when we felt it was necessary."

"Some of the boys didn't need but the one spanking; they didn't want to go back," he added. "Some of the kids, sometimes they would try to be tough."

A NEED TO HEAL

For the past several months, the Department of Juvenile Justice has been torn over what to do for the White House boys. Now in their 60s, they say the events of a half-century ago forever shaped their lives—and not for the better.

"Our hearts go out to these men," DJJ Secretary Frank Peterman told *The Miami Herald*. "We certainly want them to understand that we want them to be healed."

Peterman, also a St. Petersburg Baptist minister, also wants them to know the state's juvenile lock-ups—and Dozier in particular—are far different places from what they once were. "We just don't tolerate the maiming or abuse of kids," he said.

"We just want to bring closure to a very tragic time in our state."

The state banned corporal punishment—including the strap—at places like Dozier in 1967. But the department continued to be rocked by scandals after the deaths of children in the state's care, including a Miami boy who died of appendicitis in 2003 after begging guards for medical help.

The Florida Times Union, in June 1899, called the reformatory "a new departure in the treatment of youthful criminals."

It was tucked amid the forests of rural Jackson

County amid 1,200 acres of pristine land. By the turn of the century, the state had built two brick dormitories a half-mile apart—one for the white children, the other for "coloreds." There was corn and sugar cane and peas and velvet beans and cotton and hogs and mules, and a brick-making factory for the youths to learn a trade.

But by 1903, the lofty experiment already had gone horribly wrong. "We found them in irons, just like common criminals, which in the judgment of your committee is not the meaning of a state reform school," a Senate inspection committee wrote, calling the school "nothing more nor less than a prison."

Seven years later, a special legislative committee reported that "the inmates were at times unnecessarily and brutally punished, the instrument of punishment being a leather strap fastened to a wooden handle." The lawmakers were assured that the beatings ended with the firing of a superintendent.

DEADLY BLAZE

In November 1914, a fire erupted in a "broken and dilapidated" stove in the white boys' dormitory while many of the guards had been visiting a house of ill repute in town, a grand jury reported. Six boys died.

By law, the white and black children were housed in camps a half-mile apart, and were forbidden to come in contact at any point. The camps were separate, but decidedly not equal.

Reports by lawmakers in 1911 and 1913 described the white inmates' quarters as "neatly kept," housing "comfortably clad" and "happy" children.

The "Negro School," however, was "more in the nature of a convict camp."

As a rule, the report said, the black children were "kept at work the entire day," only to return at night to a dormitory where they slept two to a bed in cots without mattresses. "The sleeping quarters are very poorly ventilated, and, crowded as they are, must necessarily be injurious to the health of the inmates."

REPUTATION GROWS

For decades, the Marianna reform school was a powerful symbol of the force Florida would bring to bear against youngsters who broke the law—or simply refused to conform. Records show that run-aways, truants and "incorrigibles" often found themselves locked within the same walls as car thieves and assailants.

"When kids were growing up, their parents would say to them, "If you don't behave, we'll send you to Dozier," said the current superintendent, Mary Zahasky. "This happened all over the state."

Harsh treatment and outright beatings were not uncommon in lockups and youth camps throughout the United States, especially in the middle of the 20th century, but at Dozier, they "were beyond the pale," said Ronald Davidson, director of the University of Illinois at Chicago's Mental Health Policy Program.

"These were organized, government-approved—and certainly government-ignored—systems of gratuitous cruelty," said Davidson, who has overseen troubled juvenile justice and child welfare programs for 25 years for both the Illinois state and federal governments.

North of U.S. 90 in the county seat, the reform school is set amid a landscape of red clay, green grass, and thick stands of oak and pine. In the

1950s and 1960s, it held dormitories of red and whitewashed brick next to ramshackle cracker houses of concrete and stucco.

"When I arrived there, I was quite impressed," said Straley. 'It was a beautiful place. The cottages were all brick and the bushes were trimmed, there were big oak trees and it was beautifully landscaped and I thought, 'Wow, this is really something. I might make some friends here and have a good time.'"

But there was something awful beyond the first impression.

"You just knew this is not a college campus, and these kids are not having a good time," said Michael O'McCarthy, who went by his stepfather's surname of Babarsky during his childhood. "You just got the sense there is something wrong. Call it foreboding."

"You just knew then you had found a new kind of hell."

A yellowing official binder filled with old-fashioned cursive notes Michael Babarsky's correctional journey in dispassionate details: His inmate number is 27719. He is the son of A.J. and Edna Babarsky of Islamorada. He was sentenced to the reform school by Judge Eva Gibson for stealing and running away "until legally discharged."

CONSEQUENCES

O'McCarthy entered the camp on May 14, 1958, escaped July 7, 1958, and was recaptured the next day.

O'McCarthy said he was warned that running from the camp would fetch dire consequences. And some of the tougher boys wore the consequences like a badge of honor. "How many did you get?" they'd be asked as they hobbled back to their cottages from The White House, their bottoms bruised and bloodied under their cotton trousers.

The first thing most of the White House boys remember is the fan. It hung from the ceiling in a corridor, an industrial-sized contraption that sounded like a roaring engine. The guards apparently were trying to prevent the boys waiting in line for beatings from panicking, hoping the noise would drown out the thwack-thwack-thwack of the strap and the anguished screams. It didn't.

"I was so scared, I begged Jesus to take me out of

this world," said Bill Haynes, who was at the reform school from April 11, 1958, to Nov. 29, 1959. "I think everybody finds Jesus in that place." Haynes is now communications director for the Alabama prison system, and a former prison guard.

Said Straley: "You were terrified. It's the most scared I've ever been."

GRIM RITUAL

The boys were told to lie on their bellies and grip the metal railing at the head of a bunk bed. The mattress was covered with blood and body fluids. The pillow smelled like body odor, and was flecked with tiny pieces of human tongues and lips from when boys bit themselves, said Richard Colon, 65, a Hialeah boy who was sent to the school on May 17, 1957, for stealing cars. He now lives in Baltimore.

The strap was kept under the pillow. "It was attached to a wooden handle," said Straley, 64. "These guys really knew how to use it, and they prided themselves on that fact. They could bring blood with one blow."

The boys would be told, they now say, that the whipping would stop if they squirmed or screamed or tried to jump off the cot, and when it resumed, it would start all over from the beginning. The boys never knew how many licks they were getting until it was over.

"I think the reason they didn't want you to scream was because it got to them," said O'McCarthy.

'THE ONE-ARMED MAN'

Five men interviewed by *The Miami Herald* recall being whipped by two men: Robert Hatton, an assistant superintendent who is deceased, and Tidwell, who accidentally severed his left arm with a shotgun when he was 6. The men still refer to him as "the one-armed man."

Hatton, who did most of the beatings, would jerk and pivot on the concrete floor like a pitcher every time he raised and lowered the belt, Haynes said.

When the leather hit its mark, they say, the little army cot would heave and converge, sometimes a foot at a time. The first two or three cracks were easy. But then the reality sank in.

"I couldn't believe I was being hit with that much force," said Straley. "When they were hitting you in the same spot and they had already broken the skin or bruised you, you were in some serious pain. I went out of there in shock."

Colon, who said he was only 14 and weighed less than 100 pounds, still can feel the fury. "I can tell you that at that moment, there's absolutely no doubt in my mind, I could have stuck my hand through his heart and his chest cavity and ripped his heart out with my hand and bit it in his face," he said.

Some of the boys had to be taken to an infirmary to have small pieces of cotton underwear extracted from their buttocks with tweezers and surgical tools, they said.

"Your hind end would be black as a crow," said Haynes. "It had a crust over it. Your shorts will be embedded into your skin and would have to be pulled out. And when they pulled them out, it hurts even worse."

Though such beatings and abuse often were justified under a "patina of social beliefs" that physical discipline could rehabilitate troubled children, Davidson said, decades of academic research has made clear that such punishment serves no real purpose.

"Everything we know about psychological trauma in abused and neglected children tells us that this will create a lifelong emotional scar which will color every aspect of childhood and adult development," Davidson said.

In recent months, some of the White House alumni discovered one another through the gripping narratives they had posted on Internet blogs. A handful will deliver brief statements in front of The White House on Tuesday, before DJJ administrators dedicate a commemorative plaque and plant a symbolic tree.

After the ceremony, the men plan to visit a small clearing apart from the new Dozier, in a remote corner of what used to be the black children's campus, where a cemetery with the graves of 32 who died there sits—including the victims of the 1914 fire. The graves are marked by unadorned metal pipe crosses—but bear no names.

The men say they pushed memories of the White House as far back as their minds would let them. Some of the men say they fought episodes of anger and rage, but mostly went about living their lives. Some of the men have sought counseling, they say.

'THERE FOREVER'

Roger Kiser, a Georgia man who was taken to the reformatory on June 3, 1959, has been married six times, divorced five times. He said he had trouble expressing love, though he finally got the hang of it when he became a grandfather.

Straley, the Clearwater man, said he has rationed the time he spends out of his house since he began trembling one day at a Wal-Mart, prompting another shopper to ask him what was wrong.

It took the videotaped death of a 14-year-old Panama City boy, Martin Anderson, at a state juvenile boot camp in 2006 to bring the memories flooding back. Though the two would have had nothing in common, Straley said he felt a sudden surge of anger, clenched his fists and cussed—much as Martin might have done.

"The thing is in your head fresh as a daisy," Straley said. "That feeling is there forever."

Said Colon, the Hialeah boy who returns to Dozier yearly to hand out scholarships to current detainees: "You don't get over it. You learn how to bear pain."

Appendix V. News Article on Unmarked Graves

Unknown graves at Fla. reform school investigated

By BRENDAN FARRINGTON
Associated Press Writer

TALLAHASSEE, Fla. (AP)—A former inmate at a Florida reform school known for severe beatings decades ago says he remembers walking into a laundry room, peering through a foggy dryer window and seeing a boy tumbling inside. Afraid of retribution, Dick Colon walked away.

But Colon now wonders whether the boy he saw could be buried near the school. Florida law enforcement said Tuesday they have started an investigation into the enduring mystery: Who lies beneath the more than 30 white metal crosses—bearing no names or dates or other details—at a makeshift cemetery near the grounds of the Arthur G. Dozier School for

Boys, where youngsters were routinely beaten and abused in the 1950s and '60s.

"I think about it very often because I feel guilty. I felt as though I could have walked over there and opened the door and tried to give him some help, but then what the hell was going to happen to me if I did?" said Colon, now 65 and living in Baltimore. "That particular kid was never seen again."

Gov. Charlie Crist ordered the Florida Department of Law Enforcement to investigate at the urging of Colon and other men who committed crimes as boys and were sent to the school. The agency was tapped to find out what was in the graves, identify any remains and determine whether any crimes occurred.

"Justice always cries out for a conclusion and this is no different," Crist told reporters. "If there's an opportunity to find out exactly what happened there, to be able to verify if there were these kinds of horrible atrocities ... we have a duty to do so."

The Department of Juvenile Justice has no records that explain what's in the cemetery near the 108-year-old reform school.

One theory is the graves contain the bodies of six boys who died in a 1914 school fire. But that would only explain a fraction of the markers.

Current school superintendent Mary Zahasky hopes the graves do not contain children.

"When I first saw it—those kinds of things tug at your heart. I'm a mother myself," she said. "I just can't imagine having my child buried out there like that."

Colon is part of a group of men who call themselves "The White House Boys Survivors" because they suffered abuse in a small, white building known as the White House. It contained two rooms where guards would beat children, one for black inmates; one for whites.

The boys were forced to lie on a bed, face down in a pillow covered with blood, spit and mucous, and were repeatedly struck with a long leather-and-metal strap for offenses as slight as singing, or talking to a black inmate. They described beatings so severe that underwear became imbedded in skin.

The Department of Juvenile Justice acknowledged the abuse in October, placing a plaque on the now-closed white building.

"The staff was so brutal that just even the slightest frown on your face or even the slightest word out of context could cause you to be sent down to the White

House and be viciously beaten to the point that you would become unconscious and bleed profusely down your legs and your back," Bryant Middleton, 63, of Fort Walton Beach, said Monday.

After the October ceremony, Department of Juvenile Justice staff took five of the former inmates to the cemetery, which is located near the facility that used to house black inmates. An adult prison now stands on the property.

"This is a big occasion for the state of Florida," Michael O'McCarthy, 66, who was sent to the detention center when he was 15 for stealing auto parts, said of the investigation. "Rarely do state or federal governments like to admit that they have committed this type of egregious, destructive kinds of crimes, especially to children."

At least one former reform school student said the men's stories may be exaggerated.

"They were justified in giving me these paddlings because, hey, I was wrong," said Phil Hail of Anniston, Ala., who remembered going to the white building once for getting low grades in 1957. "It comes down to if you abide by the rules, you're not punished."

Hail's description was similar to what the other

men described, but he said the school wasn't a "house of horrors."

"Was (the school) run with a very strict hand? Yes, it was," he said. "Were the paddlings very severe? Yes, they were."

Appendix VI. OP-ED Article on Memories of State Abuse

http://tallahassee.com/article/20081023/OPINION01/810230307

Our Opinion: Memories of state abuse can't be erased

In the 1950s and '60s, the Florida State Reform School in Marianna, where many young male offenders wound up, had a notorious reputation. Backyard scuttlebutt, especially among teenagers, is often wildly exaggerated, so the tales of terrible beatings were easily dismissed. After all, they came from young men whose credibility was unreliable to begin with.

They weren't exaggerating.

In an emotional ceremony Tuesday on the grounds of the institution now known as the Arthur G. Dozier School for Boys, the Department of Juvenile Justice, which oversees the facility, acknowledged the horrific abuse.

State officials invited five men—they call themselves the "White House Boys" after the whitewashed
cinderblock building where they were mercilessly
beaten—to attend a two-hour ceremony at which
they were allowed to make uncensored statements
about their experiences. Healing was the goal.

Mike McCarthy, 65, recalled "blood spattered all
over the walls."

Associated Press reporter Brendan Farrington covered the event. He described "a dark room barely big
enough to fit the bed (Mike McCarthy) and other children lay in while they were beaten so badly he said
some had to have underwear surgically removed."

Roger Kiser, 62, was sent to the reform school
after running away from an orphanage in Jacksonville where he was being molested. He said
when he got to Marianna, he realized he was better
off at the orphanage. The Associated Press picks up
his account.

"When I walked out of this building . . . when I
looked in the mirror, I couldn't tell who I was, I was
so bloodied. From that day forward, I've never forgotten what rotten SOBs the human being can be.

"Nobody treated me with respect, I was nothing

more than a dog," he said. "I certainly hope things have changed. I pray to God."

In the building across from the White House, the victims said, was what they called the rape room.

"They were monsters," 62-year-old Robert Straley of Clearwater said of the state employees who abused him. "Oh my God, the things they did."

After all five men spoke, Gus Barreiro, a former lawmaker who now oversees DJJ's residential programs, unveiled a plaque outside the White House.

"In memory of the children who passed through these doors, we acknowledge their tribulations and offer our hope that they found some measure of peace. May this building stand as a reminder of the need to remain vigilant in protecting our children as we help them seek a brighter future."

It is rare for a government agency to acknowledge even errors of policy, but more rare to acknowledge such dire human behavior stemming from judgments that one can only assume started from the top. This week's acknowledgment improves the credibility of DJJ, of course, and the public can only hope that such horrors are now truly part of the past.

Appendix VII. A Brief History of the Facility

From the Florida Archives

Before the official opening of The Florida State Reform School on January 1, 1900, Florida counties had very few outlets for troubled youths. Lawmakers had hoped that this institution and others like it would provide proper housing, education, employment, and rehabilitation for children who were convicted of illegal activities or were merely dependents of the state. Although the initial intention was good, the execution of the plan failed miserably. Life at the school was often brutal; in 1903, a legislative committee reported that it found "[inmates] in irons, just as common criminals," and in 1911, a report of a special joint committee on the reform school said, "the inmates were at times unnecessarily and brutally punished, the instrument of punishment being a leather strap fastened to a wooden handle."

The leasing out of convicts for free labor was traditional during this era, but not all the children living at these institutes were convicted criminals: many were simply wards of the state. It was reported on a number of occasions that these children, some not even twelve years of age, were forced to perform to the same standards set for their adult counterparts. Those who failed to meet these standards received severe beatings. This was confirmed in 1911 by the legislative committee hired to report on the living conditions at the school. The ages of the children ranged from nine to eighteen years old. However, counties had jurisdiction to hold anyone up to the age of twenty-one. Many of the boys were treated as hardened criminals and served on chain gangs, which were frequently used during the 1920s as a way to maintain control over a group of convicts. Boys were shackled together to prevent them from escaping or overpowering their guards.

At a state convict camp in Orange County in 1921, two of the thirty-six young workers assigned to the road construction crew refused to work, which resulted in severe beatings for these boys. This ultimately created an uprising and commanded the attention of the Board of Commissioners of State Institutions. As if the severe beatings and poor living conditions weren't enough, a fire in November of 1914 took the lives of six of the boys and two of the school's staff members. Four years later the school suffered another major loss during the 1918 Spanish influenza epidemic.

By 1920, the Boys Industrial School in Marianna (renamed in 1913) maintained two racially separate campuses. It housed a minimum of three hundred children, even though it had been originally designed to hold only half that number. By 1926, severe overcrowding was reported and the suggested solution was to parole some of the boys in order to ease congestion. However, by the 1930s, the school was reporting a rapidly growing population and a high rate of escapes.

By 1923 Florida had been forced to abandon the convict lease system because of increased public pressure. However, many counties found the system to be far too profitable and continued to lease labor to local residents for business or individual use. It wasn't until a 1930 investigative survey of the juvenile system that Florida was required, by law, to revamp their legal proceedings of minors and bring their standards up to par with the national level.

In 1946, a former schoolteacher named Arthur G. Dozier was named as superintendent of the school, and later the school was renamed for him. It wasn't until 1982 that advocates for children and prison reform filed a statewide class-action lawsuit to reform the state's juvenile justice system. Among their allegations: children, some as young as ten, were held in severe crowding and sometimes were shackled and hogtied.

Florida's treatment of young offenders was well-documented in the 1983 class-action civil rights lawsuit, known as the Bobby M. Case. The case, brought on behalf children who were mistreated in the state's juvenile justice facilities, including Dozier, ushered in a new era of reform. At Dozier, the atrocities documented included the actions of the "dog boys," a group of guards who used attack dogs on the boys. It is reported that the late Louis de la Parte, the crusading former state senator from Tampa, personally saw the blood-splattered "White House" building where vicious beatings had occurred.

In 1987, after a four-year legal battle with the state, another overhaul of the youth corrections system was mandated. Then, in October 2008, the Florida State Department of Juvenile Justice dedicated a plaque outside the white cinder-block building in the rear of the Dozier School for Boys where they have acknowledged that boys incarcerated at the facility had been beaten. The doors to the White House were to be closed forever.

In December 2008, the governor called for an investigation into allegations of child abuse and possible homicides at the school during the 1950s and 60s. At the center of the investigation are the unmarked graves of unknown persons, marked only by crude white crosses.

___

SOURCES: http://etd.lib.fsu.edu/theses/available/etd-10252005-172103/unrestricted/ Main_Dissertation.pdf; Florida Times Union Governor's Letters and Correspondence, Letter from W. S. Jennings to Board of Commissioners of Duval County January 30, 1902, p 432; Minutes of the Board of Commissioners of Marion County, August 8, 1905, p 2; , April 5, 1901, np; Carper, "Convict-Lease," p 209; The Marianna Times Courier "House Journal, 1905, Governor's message, pp 15-16; , March 10, 1905, np.; *www2.tbo.com/content/2008/dec/15/na-state-right-to-raise-ghosts-of-dozier-schools-p/*; Juvenile Courts, p 31; Schlotterback, Darrell Louis, "A Study of the Pre-Institutional Background and Institutional Conformity of Eighty Students At the Florida School for Boys at Marianna," Masters Thesis, Florida State University, 1961, pg. 26; New York Herald Samuel McCoy Papers, "Concurrent Resolution on Tabert Affair" passed by North Dakota Legislature, February 27, 1923; March 8, 1923, np; Gudmunder Grimson Papers.

About The White House Boys Organization

I have worked for many years to try to expose the horrors that I and many others experienced at the Florida Industrial School for Boys at Marianna. Then one day, I reached for the ringing telephone, and, finally, all hell was about to break loose on the State of Florida.

"Is this Roger Kiser, the fellow who wrote the stories about the White House at Marianna?" a gentleman asked.

After I confirmed that I was Roger Kiser, the gentlemen told me his girlfriend had come across my stories on the Internet and that he had also been at the school. That call compelled me to build the website "The Horrors of the White House-FSB Marianna." Through various websites and message boards, I was able to reach more men who had been beaten and abused at the hands of the State of Florida. Through these connections, "The White House Boys" organization was formed. Hundreds of calls and emails started pouring in, telling us of the horrors, rapes, beatings, and murders of hundreds of boys over the past fifty years.

We have come along way in seeing justice served, but we still have far to go. Due to different ideas on how to proceed now that an investigation is underway, our organization has split into two separate entities, with each proceeding in the manner they feel best to accomplish the difficult tasks at hand. God speed to us all.

Visit us at WWW.THEWHITEHOUSEBOYS.COM.

About Roger Dean Kiser

Roger Dean Kiser's stories take you into the heart of a child abandoned by his mother and abused by the system responsible for his care. In a style reminiscent of Mark Twain, Roger Dean Kiser's collection of almost 1,000 stories capture the drama and emotion of a sad, lonely, and confused childhood as well as the heartwarming views and emotions of a kind man who truly understands how precious life is. Kiser's writing carries with it strong images and feelings that search out and find that thread inside that connects each of us to our own emotions.

Kiser's stories have been published in books and magazines around the world, including *Heartwarmers, Heartwarmers of Love, Chicken Soup for the*

Grandparent's Soul, Chicken Soup for the Horse Lover's Soul, Chicken Soup for the Caregiver's Soul, Chicken Soup for the Friend's Soul, Chicken Soup for the Dog Lover's Soul, Chicken Soup for the Cat Lover's Soul, Chicken Soup for the Grandma's Soul, and *Chicken Soup for the Adopted Soul.*

Kiser's short story "The Bully" was made into a short film by Executive Producer Edward Asner and has been entered into several major film festivals in the United States.

Kiser lives in Brunswick, Georgia, with his wife, Judy, where he continues to write and spend time with his family.

Visit him at www.RogerDeanKiser.com.

"Well, Toto, I guess we're not in Kansas anymore."

Courage to Survive

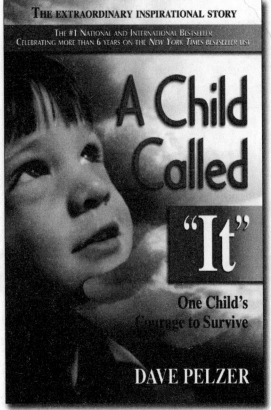